BLITZ THE BIG BOOK OF CARTOONING

THE ULTIMATE
GUIDE TO HOURS
AND HOURS
OF FUN CREATING
FUNNY FACES,
WACKY CREATURES,
AND LOTS MORE!

By
BRUCE
BLITZ

RUNNING PRESS
PHILADELPHIA • LONDON

9   8   7   6   5
Digit on the right indicates the number of this printing

Library of Congress Cataloging-in-Publication Number 97-66804

ISBN 0-7624-0939-8

Cover design by Paul Kepple
Interior design by Corinda Cook and Terry Peterson
Edited by Greg Jones
Set in Comic and Univers

Published by Courage Books, an imprint of
Running Press Book Publishers
125 South Twenty-second Street
Philadelphia, Pennsylvania 19103-4399

If you are interested in ordering Bruce Blitz Video Kits, please visit your local

arts and crafts store, or send for a video kit catalog:

Blitz Art Products

P.O. Box 8022

Cherry Hill, NJ 08002

USA

CONTENTS

ACKNOWLEDGEMENTS

I wish to thank my lovely wife, Frances, and my incredible children, Alanna and Eric, for being my loving and supportive family. My terrific parents Sarah and Bill for accepting that they raised a cartoonist. Also, my creative sister Adrienne, who used to teach me how to draw when I was a boy. A special thanks to all the great cartoonists whose artwork inspired me to follow my dreams. Above all, I thank God, from whom all talent comes.

ABOUT THE AUTHOR

Bruce Blitz started out as the boy who drew funny pictures of the principal at school. Now he appears at numerous school assembly programs and demonstrates his cartooning skills to rave reviews (including the principal!). He has been drawing professionally for more than 20 years.

Blitz is the creator and host of the internationally aired television series *Blitz on Cartooning*, which has earned four Emmy Award nominations. He has authored several instructional books on drawing, produced a series of instructional drawing videos, and has appeared on a bunch of television programs, including *The Joan Rivers' Show*, Discovery Channel's *Start to Finish*, and the QVC Shopping Network. Blitz is mostly self-taught, thanks to his experience in a wide variety of artistic fields. He has operated his own animation company in Philadelphia and Las Vegas, where he produced cartoon television commercials and animated sequences.

An accomplished, professional musician performing on both piano and organ, Blitz wrote the music for his television show and all of his instructional videos. The music from *Blitz on Cartooning* was even nominated for an Emmy! He is also noted for his caricature work, having appeared nationwide at trade shows, conventions, vacation resorts, and the 1982 World's Fair in Knoxville, Tennessee.

He was born in Philadelphia, Pennsylvania, and now resides in Cherry Hill, New Jersey with his wife and two children.

FOREWORD

As an established syndicated cartoonist, the last thing I'm looking for is young, fresh competition. The author of this book, through his TV shows and videos, has launched untold aspiring creators onto the market. This obviously will edge some of us old-timers off the comics page and out of business.

Several years ago I was personally blitzed by Blitz during a joint appearance on a TV talk show. He drew a very funny caricature of me that had everybody laughing. Except me! What a blatantly insulting portrait.

And now this same Blitz guy has the nerve to ask me to write the foreword for his book!

Well, "The Family Circus" has a reputation for being sincere and honest. I am therefore obliged to give a frank evaluation of "The Big Book of Cartooning."

It is a brilliant compilation of the many basic aspects of drawing, simplified and presented in a breezy, entertaining style. I only wish it had been available when I was in high school trying to teach myself to draw.

Good luck to all you fledgling artists as you add your manpower (and woman power) to the many newcomers hoping to bump poor little Billy, Dolly, Jeffy, and PJ out of the newspapers, into the streets to fend for themselves.

And remember: Self-esteem is important to success. So don't let Bruce Blitz draw your caricature.

Bil Keane
Creator of *The Family Circus*

INTRODUCTION

Have you ever found yourself creating works of art in the margin of your notebook? How about the telephone book or shopping lists—are they covered with drawings, too? Well, if you are one of those people who can't stop doodling, you are not alone. And I've got good news for you—this book can help you turn those doodles into finished cartoons!

What are cartoons, anyway? They are simply drawings that express a funny idea. We enjoy cartoons because they can take us away from our problems; they illustrate our fantasies and poke fun at everyday situations.

When you draw cartoons, you are the boss and you decide everything! You create the main character, set up the gag, draw the supporting cast of characters, design the props (all the items that surround the characters), and choose the "camera angle."

And remember, if you always assumed that great cartoonists are lucky because they were just born with talent, don't believe it! While it's true that some people may have been born with a bit more talent than others, anyone with a pencil, paper, and desire can become a good cartoonist. All it takes is imagination and practice.

So sit back, relax, and let your mind go—because anything is possible in the world of cartooning!

ART SUPPLIES

All you really need to get started
drawing Blitz cartoons is:
1) Pencil
2) Paper
3) Eraser
4) Marker

PENCILS

For cartooning, I prefer to use an HB or a No. 2 pencil. HB refers to the softness of the lead—the higher the number, the softer the lead. An HB pencil, which can be found in art stores, is a more professional version of the No. 2 pencil, which is used in schools and is available anywhere. Both of these pencils are great for sketching and laying out your cartoon. A 2B or 3B pencil works well for shading because the lead is softer. But watch out!—they will smear more easily, too. 2B or not 2B . . . let's just say that HB and No. 2 pencils are good all-around sketching pencils!

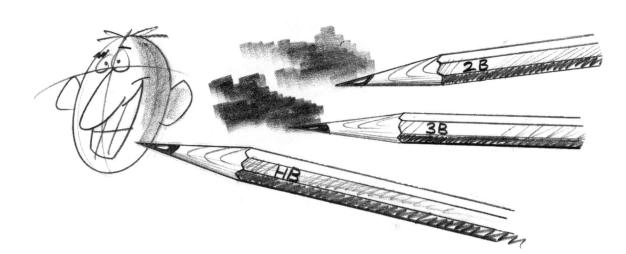

PAPER

There are many paper surfaces available that come in pads or in individual sheets. They each offer different qualities for various media, such as pencil, marker, pen and ink, and so on. Just go to an art store, look around, and experiment.

But remember, while you learn you are going to use a lot of paper. To begin with, I suggest you buy a relatively inexpensive pad of newsprint or drawing paper. Later on you can buy more expensive drawing surfaces for your finished cartoons.

COPY MACHINE PAPER

Here's what works well for me: a ream of 20# bond paper is in-expensive and available at office supply outlets, stationery stores, discount stores . . . just about anywhere. I use it all the time.

COQUILLE BOARD

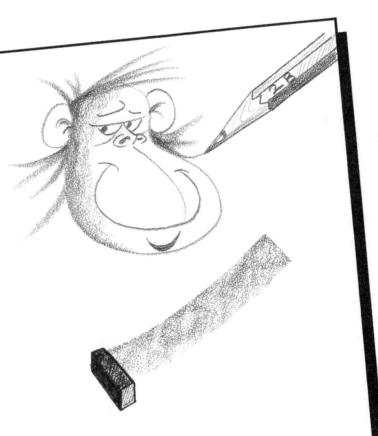

This drawing was done with a 2B pencil on coquille board, which is a rough-textured paper available in individual sheets. By laying a soft lead pencil or crayon on its side, you can achieve an interest-ing shading effect, which easily can be reproduced by photocopy. This paper is a bit more expensive than regular drawing paper.

ERASERS

Generally, any kind of eraser can be used. I prefer a kneaded rubber eraser because it can be shaped to erase in small areas by kneading it like a piece of dough or clay. By doing this, it even cleans itself. And best of all, it doesn't leave messy crumbs.

A kneaded rubber eraser looks like this when you buy it . . . and like this after you use it!

LOOK, NEXT IS MARKERS!

MARKERS

Once your cartoon is penciled in and you have made all the necessary changes, you may want to go over it with a marker. This way your cartoon will stand out with one clean, black line. By using more or less hand pressure, you can achieve some variation of line—but be careful! Some brands of markers are different than others. They vary in point size, shape, and flexibility. Most markers, however, do not hold their points for very long and won't give you a consistent line. Experiment with a few different kinds and use the ones that work best for you.

Here are some examples of the different media that are available, and the different effects which they produce. Notice the differences in the resulting lines.

LARGE POINT MARKERS

These are good for working large; by bearing down you can create a broader line.

ROLLER BALL PENS

As you can see, these pens can create very thin lines. They are good for small sketches.

BLACK COLORED PENCILS

These are like regular pencils, except they're darker.

MEDIUM POINT FELT-TIP PENS

These are good all-around tools for working about this size.

PENS AND WATERPROOF INK

These create a professional look, but they require a lot of practice. Various pen points are available.

FIBER-TIP MARKER PENS

These are similar to ball point pens.

FINE-LINE FELT-TIP PENS
These are fun to doodle with!

BRUSH
Produces a thick and thin line.
Requires much practice.
Always buy the best brush available.
This is a No. 1 sable hair.

This drawing was done with a medium felt-tip pen on coquille board, which is a rough-textured paper. By laying a pencil or piece of crayon on its side, you can achieve an interesting shading effect which can be reproduced as line art.

GREASE CRAYONS
These are terrific for working large in front of an audience, such as for a cartooning demonstration. You can break them into different sizes for shading; a large piece works great for covering large areas in one sweep.

WORK AREA

The first thing to decide is where you are going to set up your work area.

The good news is that a cartoonist can work just about anywhere.

Here are some items you should consider including in your studio set-up:

A) Window

B) Adjustable Drawing Table

C) Artist Tabouret (or a file cabinet will do fine) to keep your art supplies in reach

D) Adjustable Lamp

E) Comfortable Chair

F) Radio (Music and art go great together! What more can I say!)

G) Books for reference

H) Supply of drawing paper

You can create alternatives to the adjustable drawing table. Get a piece of wood approximately 18"x 24" and sand the edges, then . . .

1. prop it up with books on a flat table at any angle you wish, or . . .

2. lean the drawing board against your lap and rest it against the table, or . . .

IT WORKS FINE!!

3. just work flat on your kitchen or dining room table. I do it all the time.

ART MORGUE

All cartoonists should keep an "art morgue." An art morgue is a collection of photographs and/or illustrations of animals, people, buildings, furniture, tools, etc., that are used for reference. For example, if you are drawing a farm scene and need to know what a tractor looks like, you look it up in your art morgue.

One good way to begin your collection is to clip photographs out of magazines and newspapers, and place them in alphabetized folders.

Or, save catalogs from department stores. They have pictures of all kinds of things—appliances, lawn mowers, beds, and much more!

MORE ART SUPPLIES

I know I told you that all you really need to get started drawing cartoons is a pencil, paper, eraser, and marker . . . and that's true. However, you will find that these tools come in handy, too:

CUTTING KNIFE

A cutting knife is handy for cutting out tiny areas, making straight cuts using a metal ruler, and for cutting tint screens and patterns (see page 24).

MASKING TAPE

REGULAR MASKING TAPE is used for taping the paper to the drawing board.
WHITE MASKING TAPE, in various widths, can be used for covering mistakes.

T-SQUARES AND ASSORTED TRIANGLES

A T-Square runs along the straight edge of your drawing board and can give you consistent parallel lines. With the triangle, you can achieve perfect right angles or can simply use it to create straight lines. Keep a ruler handy for measuring.

OPAQUE WHITE PAINT AND BRUSH

Brush over mistakes with opaque white paint. However, be careful because some markers and pens will "bleed" through; so experiment. As for the brush, it pays to buy the best. A #2 sable brush will generally serve your needs. If you take care of the brush properly—by gently rinsing and drying it after every use—it will last a long time.

TRACING PAPER

A cartoonist should never be without tracing paper. Use it to redraw your original sketch over and over again until you are satisfied with it.

PENCIL SHARPENER

Keep your pencils sharp so your drawings are sharp. An electric or battery-operated sharpener is the best, but the crank-handled or hand-held type works, too.

RUBBER CEMENT

Rubber cement is a valuable tool to bond paper to paper. You can fix mistakes by redrawing a section and cementing it on top of the original.

ADDING TINTS AND PATTERNS

Here is a very cool way to give your cartoons a professional look. These shading tints and pattern screens come in a wide variety and add the illusion of color to your black-and-white drawings. When used wisely and not over-done, it can be very effective and fun to use. Here we have the same character filled in with three of my favorite patterns.

1. Chartpak No. PT015
(medium herringbone)

2. Letratone No. LT2

3. Chartpak No. PT048

REDUCED 40%

The same characters reduced 40%. The dots, lines, and patterns are still clear and legible.
It is important when choosing screens and tints that you are aware of how much your cartoons will be reduced. Experiment to make sure that the patterns will withstand the reduction without looking mushy or nondistinct.

24

HOW TO APPLY TINT SCREENS TO YOUR CARTOONS

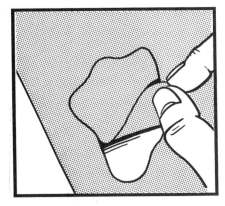

1. First, make sure you are satisfied with your drawing and that it's free of dirt or eraser crumbs. Lay a sheet of tint or pattern over the area you want to cover. You should be able to see through to your character, but if not, use your light box (see page 28).

2. Use a cutting knife to cut a piece from the sheet, but don't cut through the sheet. Tint screen sheets are adhesive, and come on protective backing. Use just enough pressure to "score" the desired area. Also, leave a bit more area around the character as shown above.

3. Next, peel the scored area off of the backing.

4. Place the piece over the cartoon, but don't press it on too hard yet. Use your knife to cut away the excess, leaving the tint or pattern where you want it. Save the excess, because it can be reused.

5. When you are finished cutting away the excess, lay a piece of clean paper over the area and rub your finger over it to make sure it bonds to your drawing.

6. Here is the final product!

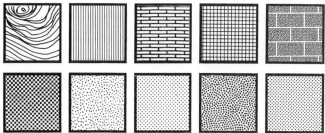

These are but a few of the many screens available. Check your local art store for more.

GRAFIX™ PAPER

THIS STUFF IS A BLAST TO USE! GRAFIX™ PAPER COMES IN MANY PATTERNS. SOME ARE UNI-SHADE (ONE PATTERN) AND OTHERS ARE DUO-SHADE (TWO PATTERNS). THE DOTS ARE ALREADY IN THE PAPER, BUT ARE INVISIBLE UNTIL YOU BRUSH ON THE DEVELOPER FLUID THAT COMES WITH THE PAPER. IT'S EASY AND IT GIVES YOUR CARTOONS A PROFESSIONAL LOOK. SO, I BRUSH AS OFTEN AS I CAN!

Actual size of original drawing

GRAFIX™ UNI-SHADE BOARD #36-D.

DEVELOPER LIQUID COMES WITH THE PAPER.

Use Grafix™ paper when a brush-effect is desired; that is, the type of effect that cannot be achieved by cutting screens.

SOME TIPS

1. Use a permanent marker or pen and ink; the developer can smear pencil lines.
2. The tendency is to overdo it; sometimes, less is more.
3. As with tint screen film, make sure your work will withstand the reduction.

Reduced by 35%

DUO-SHADE

This paper has two hidden shades that are brought out by using two different developers.

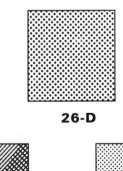

1. Draw your cartoon as before and apply developer #1 to bring up the first pattern.

   Duo-Shade #224 reduced 15% of actual size

2. Use developer #2 to bring up the second shade, which makes it appear to be darker.

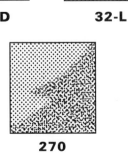

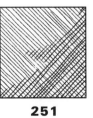

Here are some of the Uni/Duo Shades available from the Grafix™ company, which is located in Cleveland, Ohio.

UNI-SHADE

| 36-D | 26-D | 32-L | 42-L |

DUO-SHADE

| 224 | 270 | 251 |

THE LIGHTBOX

The lightbox allows you to see through 2 or 3 sheets of paper at a time. It helps you trace your rough sketches into clean lines on a new sheet.

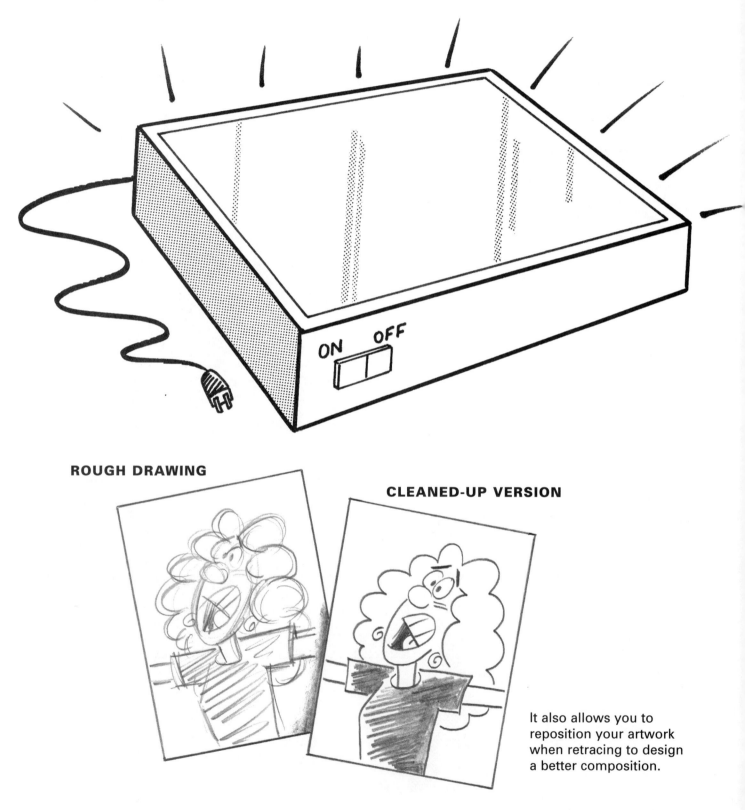

ROUGH DRAWING

CLEANED-UP VERSION

It also allows you to reposition your artwork when retracing to design a better composition.

FACE THE FACTS

IF ALL HUMANS HAVE EYES, NOSES, MOUTHS, EARS, AND BROWS, WHAT IS IT THAT MAKES US DIFFERENT FROM ONE ANOTHER? THE ANSWER IS THE SIZES, SHAPES, AND POSITION OF THE FEATURES. LET'S EXPERIMENT!

SAME FEATURES . . . DIFFERENT FACIAL OUTLINES

In the four heads above, the only differences are the outlines and hairstyles. The features are exactly the same; the eyes, nose, and mouth are spaced the same in relation to each other, yet the characters seem to be totally different.

SAME FACIAL OUTLINES . . . DIFFERENT FEATURES

These characters have the same outline and hairstyle, but different facial features. They also look very different from one another.

SAME FEATURES AND FACIAL OUTLINE . . . DIFFERENT POSITIONING

Look what happens when you "slide" around the same features inside the same face.
Experiment with this technique and see how it changes your character's character.

ALL RIGHT ALREADY! WHAT'S YOUR POINT?

IMPATIENT TYPE

MY POINT, SIMPLY, IS THAT WHEN YOU CONSIDER THE VARIOUS WAYS TO DRAW OUTLINES AND FEATURES, AND THEN APPLY THE PRINCIPLES MENTIONED ABOVE, YOU BECOME AWARE OF THE INCREDIBLE NUMBER OF COMBINATIONS THERE IS FOR CREATING CARTOON FACES. ALSO, BY ADDING ELEMENTS, SUCH AS DIFFERENT CLOTHING, BODY TYPES, ACCESSORIES LIKE GLASSES, BEARDS, MUSTACHES, HATS, FRECKLES, HAIRSTYLES, SKIN COLOR, AND AGE—NOT TO MENTION FACIAL EXPRESSIONS—THE POSSIBILITIES ARE ENDLESS!

CARTOON HEADS

Drawing cartoon heads is easy—if you take it step-by-step. We'll start by drawing a shape and adding a couple of guidelines. We will then use the guidelines to draw the features. All cartoonists work this way.

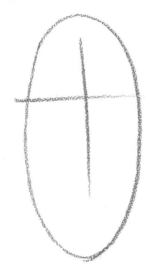   

1. Draw a shape . . . in this case, an oval. Remember to be loose. Add a vertical and horizontal guideline, as shown.

2. Using the horizontal guideline, draw two circles for the eyes and a line for the nose. The mouth can be placed any where in the rest of the shape.

3. Add the ears and more detail to the rest of the features.

4. Draw the hair and continue refining the features until you are satisfied with your cartoon head.

5. Once you have made all of your changes, you are ready to go over the sketch with your marker and draw one clean, definite line.

6. When your ink has completely dried, use your eraser and go over the entire drawing.

7. The pencil lines are gone . . . the ink lines stay . . . and there's your finished cartoon head!

HOW YA DOIN' SO FAR? LET'S TRY SOME MORE!

By varying the shape you start out with, placing the guidelines higher or lower, and changing the way you draw the features, you can make the faces look different. Always remember to start with a pencil sketch, finish with marker or ink, and then erase the pencil once the ink dries.

DIAMOND

TEARDROP

UPSIDE DOWN TEARDROP

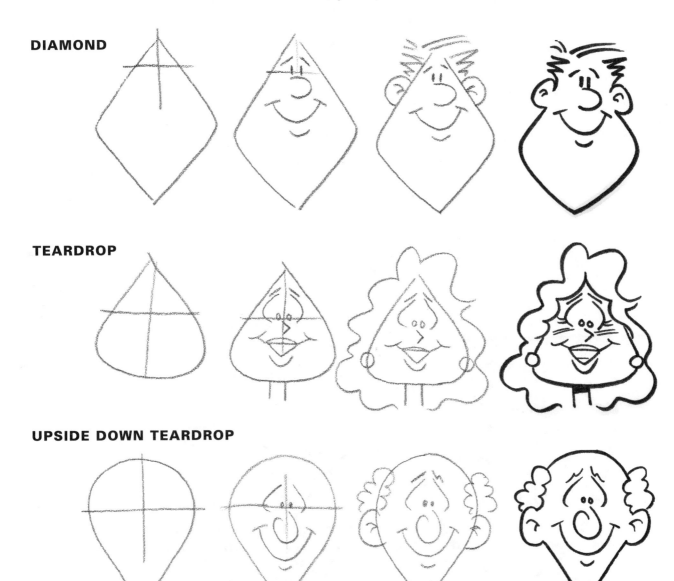

33

FACING IN DIFFERENT DIRECTIONS

This time, draw the vertical guideline a bit off to the left or the right. Now wrap that line around the oval or round shape as if it were an egg or a beach ball. Do the same thing with the horizontal guideline. Draw it in higher or lower. Draw the features as you did before and—BAM! That's how you make your cartoon heads look in different directions!

LEFT　　　　**RIGHT**　　　　**LOOKING UP**　　　　**LOOKING DOWN**

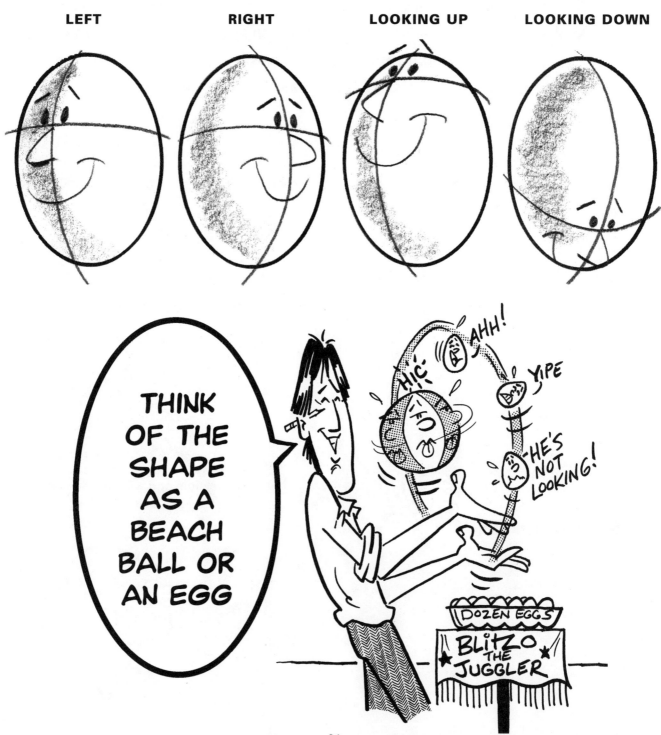

THINK OF THE SHAPE AS A BEACH BALL OR AN EGG

Once you have grasped this principle, you can have the head turning in varying degrees to just the angle you want.

HEAD TURNING

The guidelines gradually move with the direction of the head.

HEAD LOOKING UP AND TILTING BACK

Notice how the ears are lower when the head is tilted back and higher when the head is looking forward.

ALL ANGLES

Now you know how it's done, and you never have to get that wooden look for your characters again. Your cartoons can look in any direction, and will appear livelier.

MORE SHAPES, ANGLES . . . MORE CHARACTERS!

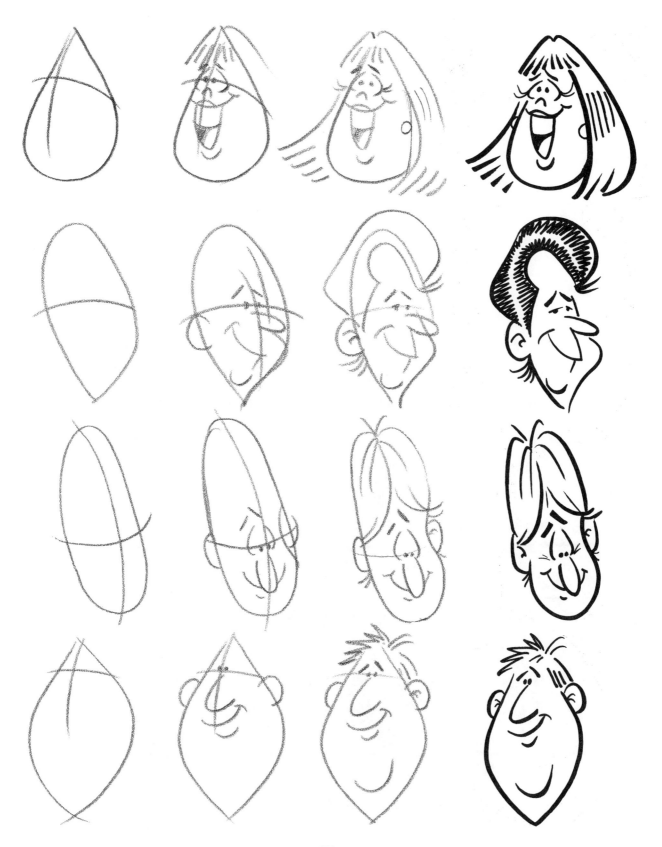

So remember, the key is to think of the shape you start
with as a three-dimensional object, such as a ball or a MELON.

There should be no shortage of three-dimensional shapes
on which to build your characters . . . just look around!

By the way, these are examples of inanimate objects coming to life. You'll learn more about this later in the book.

FEATURES

Try drawing some of these features. Practice drawing from life, but "humorize" what you see—keep the features simple and do not add too many details.

EYES

NOSES

MOUTHS

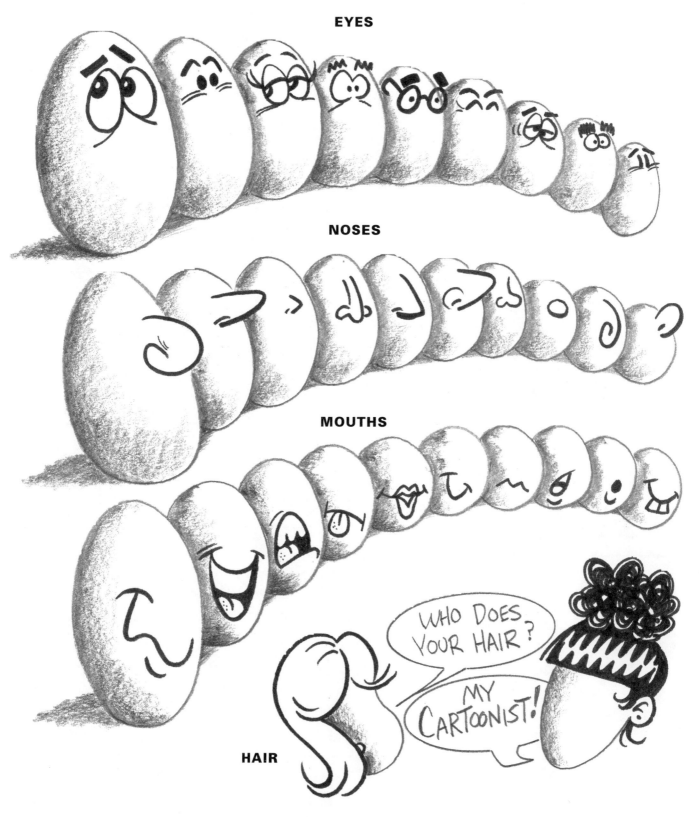

WHO DOES YOUR HAIR?

MY CARTOONIST!

HAIR

I WAS DRAWN USING A COMBINATION OF THESE FEATURES. TRY SOME OF YOUR OWN!

PRACTICE TIP #1

Draw 25 shapes
and put faces
in 'em . . .
all different.

WHEW!

Blank Expression →

ACTING CLASS TODAY 2:30

EXPRESSIONS

Now that you've learned how to create your characters, you need to put them into action! Acting is achieved by adding facial expressions. Facial expressions make your cartoons come to life; they help the characters appear to actually think. As the cartoonist, it's up to you to create the appropriate expression.

SUSPICIOUS
Eyes glancing out one side. Dotted line indicates the direction of his suspicion.

FRUSTRATION
Teeth gritting; eyebrows slanted down to indicate anger.

THINKING
One eyebrow up, the other down. Eyes looking up. Question mark and star.

STUNNED
Eyes swirling. Mouth is a broken line. Curly-cue on top indicates his head is spinning.

FEAR
Perspiration all over. He is biting his bottom lip. Eyebrows are bulging.

Many of these expressions easily could be used to illustrate other emotions. For example, "worried" could also be "nervous" or "frightened." Practice by mixing and matching features.

LAUGHING

MISCHIEVOUS

SICK

SCARED

WORRIED

SNOBBISH

SOBBING

PROUD

HYSTERICAL

CRYING

SLEEPING

Sometimes one small alteration to a feature can change the whole expression. By adding a line through the eyes, and some effects, this character's expression changes dramatically.

ALERT

DAZED

PRACTICE TIP #2

Practice by making these expressions in a mirror and transferring what you see to your paper in cartoon-style line . . . but don't get caught!

SEE MORE
CARTOON
EFFECTS AND
ACCESSORIES
ON PAGE 72.

45

CARTOON BODIES

Cartoon bodies are created in much the same way as cartoon heads—with shapes! These shapes, along with a few lines, will determine the proportions of your finished cartoon people. These are just a few of the possibilities!

"CARTOONIFIED"
This cartoon guy has fairly realistic proportions.

"REALISTIC"
The average man measures approximately 7-1/2 heads tall.

THERE ARE MANY STYLES FOR DRAWING CARTOON PEOPLE. TAKE ME, FOR EXAMPLE. I AM A SHORT, SQUAT FIGURE WITH UNREALISTIC PROPORTIONS. BUT HEY . . . I DON'T CARE!

The figure is actually made up of three-dimensional geometric forms. If that term sounds intimidating . . . don't worry. Just grasp how it looks and how the perception of depth is created.

NOTICE
HOW ONE FORM
OVERLAPS
ANOTHER FORM
IN THESE
EXAMPLES.

STEP-BY-STEP FIGURES

CYLINDER

1. Start by drawing a shape for the head and body. Use lines to indicate arms, legs, hands, and feet. This stage is to establish the character's pose. Be loose.

2. Using the guidelines, begin to "flesh out" the figure. This means to add body mass to the lines—thicken them up.

3. Refine the figure by adding clothing details. At this stage, make all the necessary changes to your cartoon.

4. Once you are satisfied with the figure, go ahead and ink it in. Once the ink dries, erase the pencil lines. After you have erased all of the pencil lines, fill in any large black areas. This is done after erasing so that you don't "gray down" the black . . . or worse, smudge it!

DIFFERENT SHAPES . . . DIFFERENT PEOPLE!

PEOPLE COME IN ALL SIZES AND PROPORTIONS . . . AND SO DO CARTOON CHARACTERS.

MOTIVATIONAL TIP

Don't look for the easy way out. The person who goes through life looking for something soft can usually find it . . . under his hat.

THIS GUY NEEDED A WHOLE PAGE FOR HIMSELF!

Look how easy
it is to turn simple
shapes into a finished
cartoon character.

SITTING POSES

WAVY LINE IN A CIRCLE

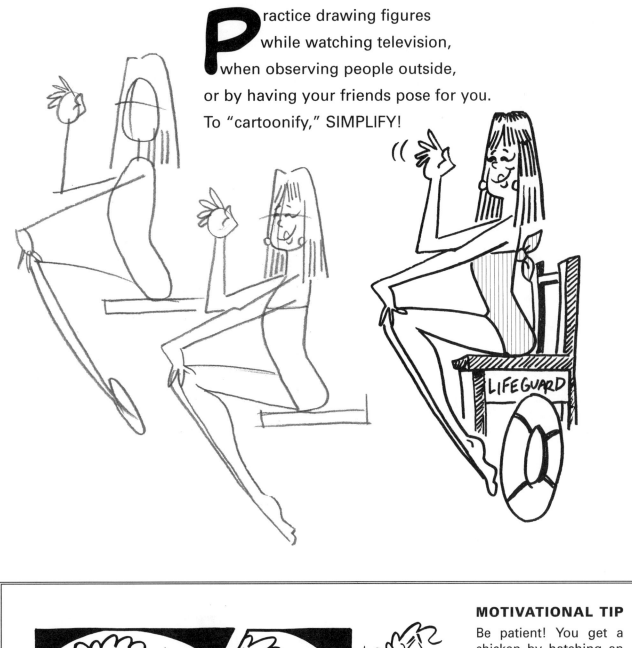

Practice drawing figures
while watching television,
when observing people outside,
or by having your friends pose for you.
To "cartoonify," SIMPLIFY!

MOTIVATIONAL TIP

Be patient! You get a chicken by hatching an egg . . . not smashing it.

53

THE WALK

BASIC SIDE VIEW

Straight Line
This figure
is happy and
walking upright.
Notice the line
of balance is vertical.

Curved Line
Nothing is going
right for this guy,
and his body
language shows it!

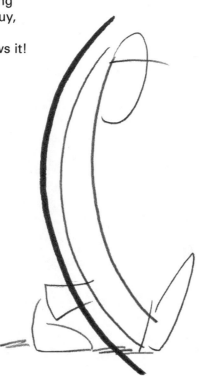

LEANING BACK

FRONT VIEW

3/4 VIEW

GOTTA PRACTICE!

55

ACTION POSES

BASIC LINE OF MOTION

When drawing a cartoon figure in action, the first step is to find what is called the basic line of motion. The best way to find this is to sketch from real people wherever you go, such as sporting events. This, too, will help sharpen your skills.

EXTREME ACTION

The most interesting way to create a character in action is to find what is known as "the extreme part of the action." For instance, this fellow is at the end of his golf swing. (Maybe the end of his career, too!)

MISSED

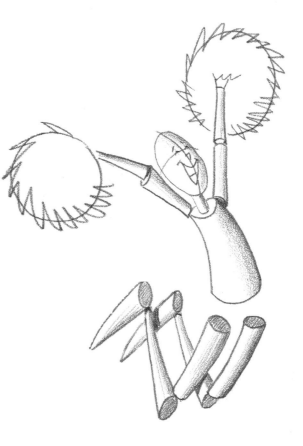

58

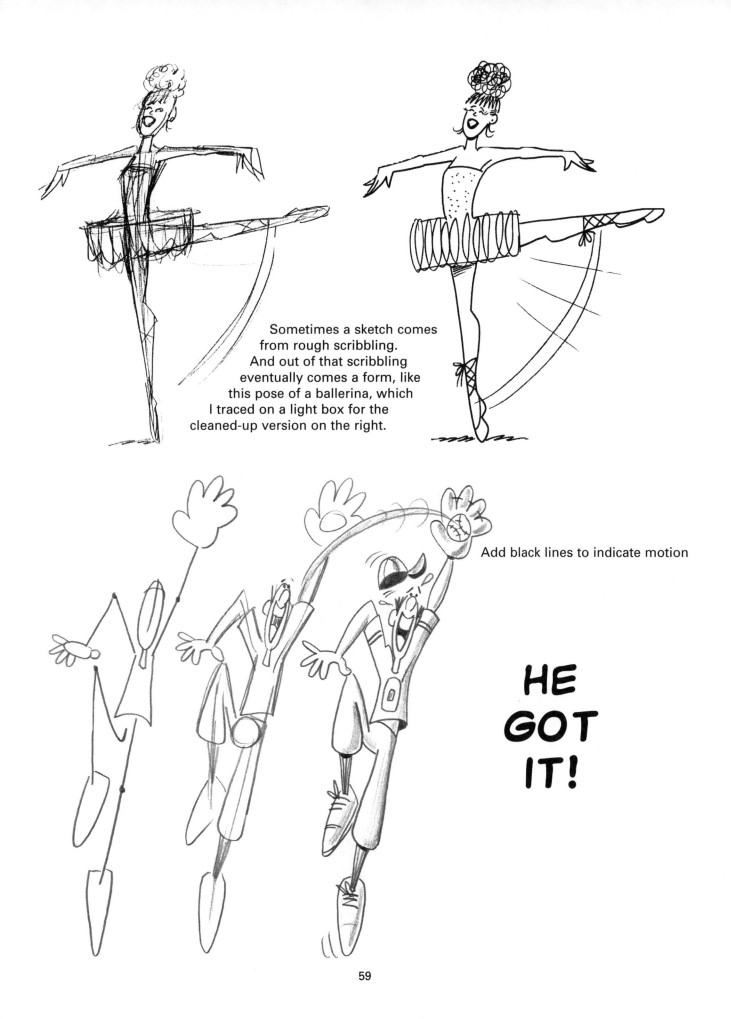

Sometimes a sketch comes
from rough scribbling.
And out of that scribbling
eventually comes a form, like
this pose of a ballerina, which
I traced on a light box for the
cleaned-up version on the right.

Add black lines to indicate motion

HE
GOT
IT!

RUNNING POSES

LEANING FORWARD

This guy is leaning forward with his back arched, and with his chest out.

A cartoonist must always have a few good running poses up his or her sleeve. They always come in handy for a good laugh in your cartoons. These running poses could be used for a chase or a race. It all depends on the facial expression and the other characters in the scene.

This character is also leaning forward, but his back is hunched forward, and yet they're both leaning-forward running poses.

LEANING BACK

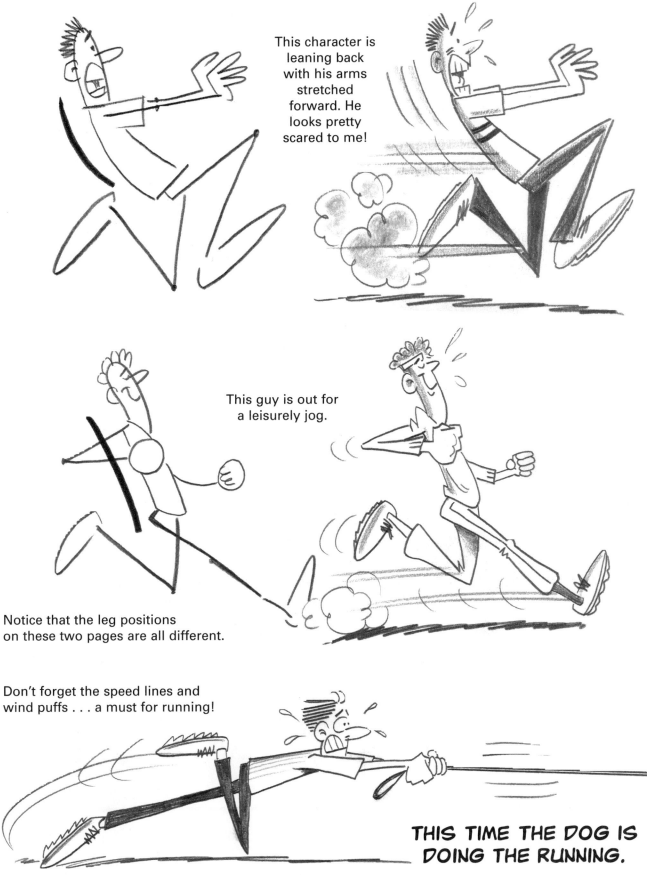

This character is leaning back with his arms stretched forward. He looks pretty scared to me!

This guy is out for a leisurely jog.

Notice that the leg positions on these two pages are all different.

Don't forget the speed lines and wind puffs . . . a must for running!

THIS TIME THE DOG IS DOING THE RUNNING.

3/4 VIEW RUNNING

See how the guidelines on this 3/4 view determine which angle the character is facing.

REAR-VIEW RUNNING

MISCELLANEOUS MUSICAL POSES

Little things, like the positioning of the legs on this singer, are valuable ingredients in creating compelling characters.

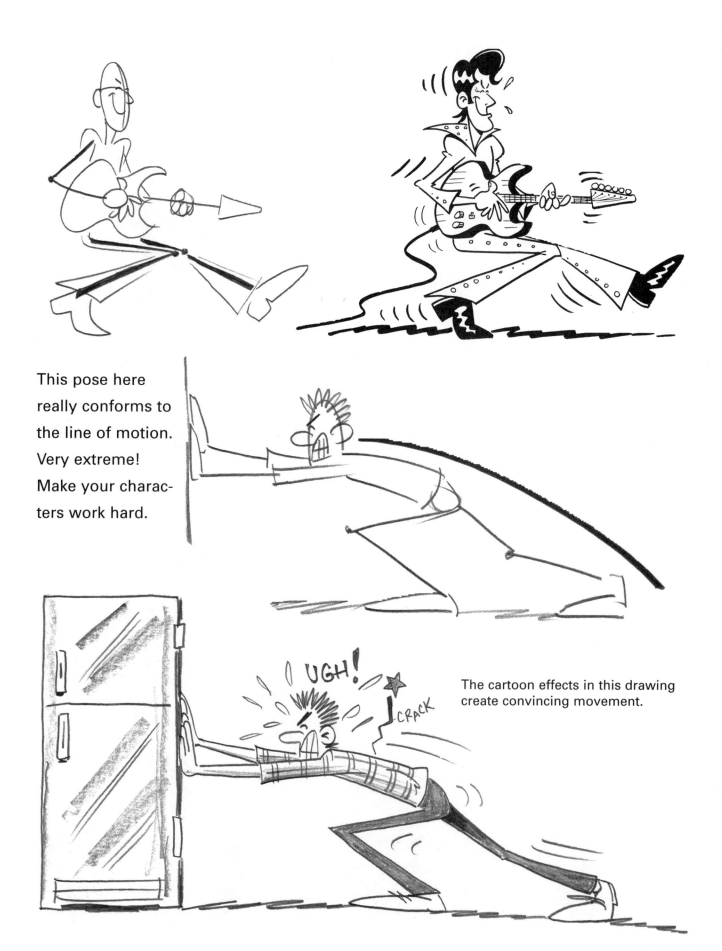

This pose here really conforms to the line of motion. Very extreme! Make your characters work hard.

The cartoon effects in this drawing create convincing movement.

A CARTOON EXERCISE

A cartoonist's job is to see humor in everyday situations—not simply to report what happens. This exercise deals with visual gags. The assignment is to take an everyday situation, like this guy below trying to buy a soda, and come up with various ways to bring humor to it.

1. In this pose here, he puts the money in and waits for the soda to come out. Not very much action here, but his facial expression sure says a lot!

2. In this drawing, he kicks the soda machine, pounds on it with his fists, and the facial expression is frustration!

3. He is now down on his knees with his arm well inside the machine. His facial expression is determination!

4. Extreme anger and frustration have taken over this guy; but his body language makes it funny, don't you think?

EMOTIONAL SITUATIONS

In this exercise, we have facial expressions linked with specific body language. There are many ways that we humans (and comic characters) can act out our emotions. Here we have only one example of each situation. If we did as many as there could be, this would be called *The Humongous Book of Cartooning*!

YOUR ASSIGNMENT IS TO COME UP WITH MORE WAYS TO USE BODY LANGUAGE WITH FACIAL EXPRESSIONS.

VERY SCARED

PLEADING

PIGGING OUT

PANIC

OVERJOYED

EXHAUSTED

SLEEPING

ANXIETY

SICK

67

HANDS

Hands are tricky to draw, but must be mastered for your characters to be complete. Here are three basic formulas for constructing a cartoon hand. Study the examples on the next two pages, and copy them over and over.

Putting fingers on a circle is one of the easiest methods.

Or try a squarish shape.

An upside-down heart.

Hands should be fairly large in relation to the rest of the figure.

The hand on the left is too small; it almost looks like a claw.

This hand works much better.

HANDS HOLD THINGS . . .

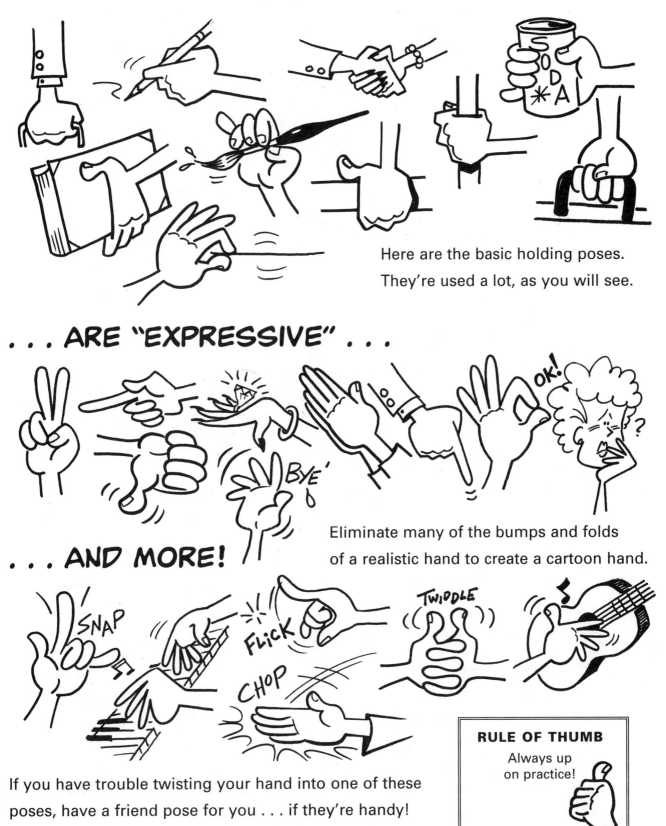

Here are the basic holding poses.
They're used a lot, as you will see.

. . . ARE "EXPRESSIVE" . . .

Eliminate many of the bumps and folds
of a realistic hand to create a cartoon hand.

. . . AND MORE!

If you have trouble twisting your hand into one of these
poses, have a friend pose for you . . . if they're handy!

RULE OF THUMB
Always up
on practice!

FEET

Feet are fun and can add a lot of humor to your cartoons. They come in various sizes, shapes, and zany styles.

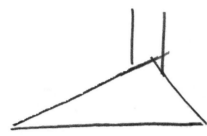

1. Start with a triangle.

2. Add some toes, an arch, and a heel.

3. Here we have a semi-realistic foot. Notice the heel protrudes backwards.

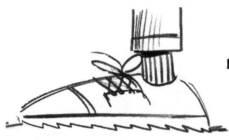

This shoe is flat on the floor. It could be considered more stylized than the next two.

DIG THOSE SOCKS!

This shoe curves up a bit, casting a shadow on the floor. This is a different style of drawing shoes.

Here's a shoe coming at you.

HERE ARE SOME EXAMPLES OF FEET WITH SHOES IN VARIOUS POSITIONS.

TAP *TAP* *TAP* *TAP*

70

SADDLE SHOES   SADDLE SHOES
                    (SMILE!)

SCREEECH

Feet—like hands—look better when drawn larger in proportion to the rest of the figure, unlike real life. It makes your cartoons funnier.

This is much better! And he looks happier, too.

MORE CARTOON EFFECTS
AND ACCESSORIES

Look for them throughout this book.

Look at this car without effects. It looks like a car just floating in the air.

Now, see what adding speed lines, smoke, dust, and sound does—the car looks like it's zooming off the page!

Some dollar signs and lines add life to this cash register.

One curly line makes this leaf look like it's gently floating with the wind.

SOME TRICKS WITH WAVY LINES

The same type of wavy lines is used in each sketch on this page,
but the lines have a different effect due to the subject of drawing.

These wavy lines convey a delicious aroma . . .

. . . and here, a "not so delicious" aroma.

The wavy lines in this case indicate heat.
Also notice how a bit of smoke,
juice from the hamburger, and a sound effect
from the burger adds to this drawing.
These effects bring the cartoon to life.

Here we have wavy lines for sound,
with a few musical notes as well.

Z-Z-Z-Z

SNORE

Two sound effects here
for this sleeping fellow.

Notice how many effects there are
in this simple drawing of two flies.

1) Lines showing path of flight.
2) A few lines showing movement of the wings.
3) Sound effect.

B-Z-Z-Z

BRRR

Shaky lines, icy breath, and a sound effect make her look chilly.
The heart in a thought balloon shows he is in love.

BONK!

A brick leaving
stars for the pain,
with the appropriate
sound effect.

Speed lines show his hair flying off.
Sweat from his face reveals how scared this
guy is. Also, notice one of the oldest
cartoon effects in the book: the little window
on his bald head, indicating the shine.

74

MORE SOUND EFFECTS

"Splat!" works well for a soft and mushy ice cream cone.

TIP

Study other cartoonists' use of effects and accessories . . . and then invent your own. It's fun to do!

"Thud!" works for a heavy book.

PRACTICE TIP #3

Take your sketch pad with you wherever you go.

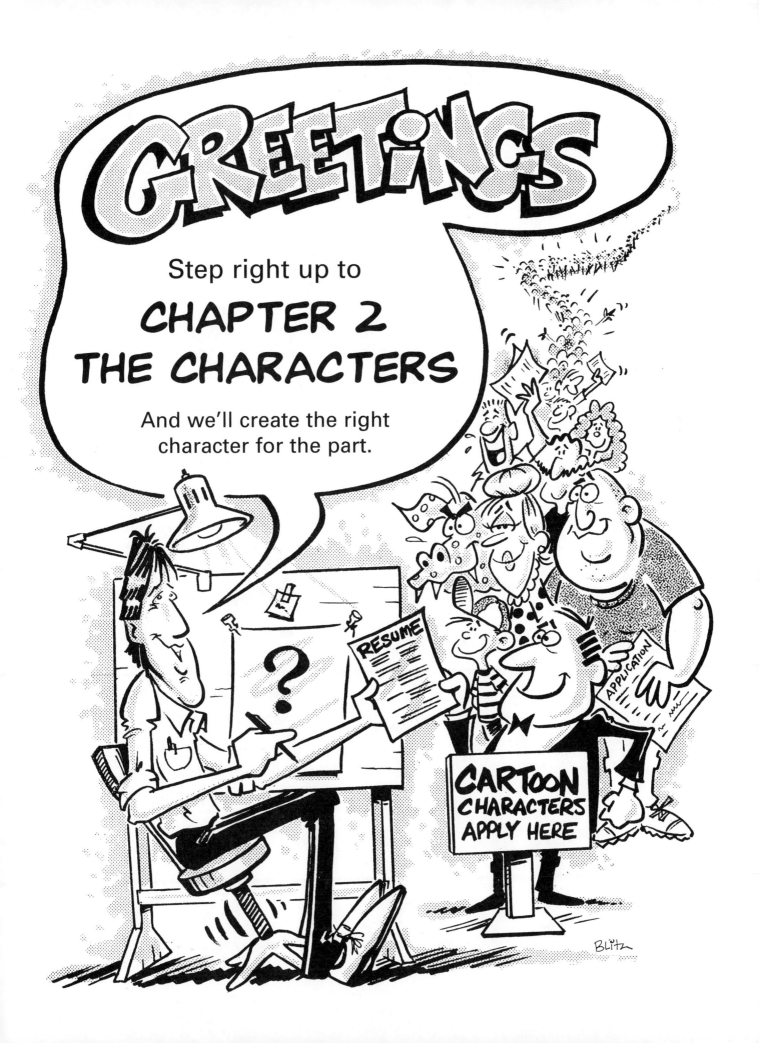

TYPICAL AVERAGE MAN

This character is the everyday "guy next door." I call him a "not too" type: not too heavy, not too thin, not too tall, not too short, and so on. This guy can be used as a family man, delivery man, mechanic, salesman, and other characters simply by changing his surroundings.

All drawings on this page were done with an HB drawing pencil.

When drawing cartoon heads, try to vary the basic shape and experiment with the placement of the guidelines. This is a great way to come up with new faces!

78

TRY TO →
VARY THE
HAIRSTYLE
FROM CHARACTER
TO CHARACTER

This fellow works well
as the guy with whom
everyone can identify.

On this page, and throughout this book, I use stick
figures for the basic construction of cartoon bodies.
However, notice how I build up the stick figure concept
by adding shapes. It is easier to get an idea of how
a figure will look by "roughing in" the general shape
of the torso; the same thing is true for hands and feet.
In some cases, shapes work better than lines (sticks)
for arms and legs. Whatever method works best for you
is, of course, what you should do. Practice by sketching
many characters in all different poses; especially action
poses. Sometimes, just a few squiggly lines are all you
need to build up your completed drawing.

TYPICAL AVERAGE WOMAN

Like the average man, this woman can be used for a wide variety of roles. The facial features and body proportions are not too extreme. By changing the costume, this everyday character could become a nurse, mom, teacher, businesswoman, etc.

TRICKS OF THE TRADE

← Use two rows of squiggly lines with a white gap between them to produce the illusion of shiny hair.

TO CREATE THE LOOK OF A POLISHED TABLE:

1. Lay your pencil on its side to add tone to the table.

2. Use an eraser to execute vertical strokes to create the reflection effect.

OLDER & LARGER WOMEN

As you can see from the examples on these two pages,
this type easily lends itself to humorous illustrations.

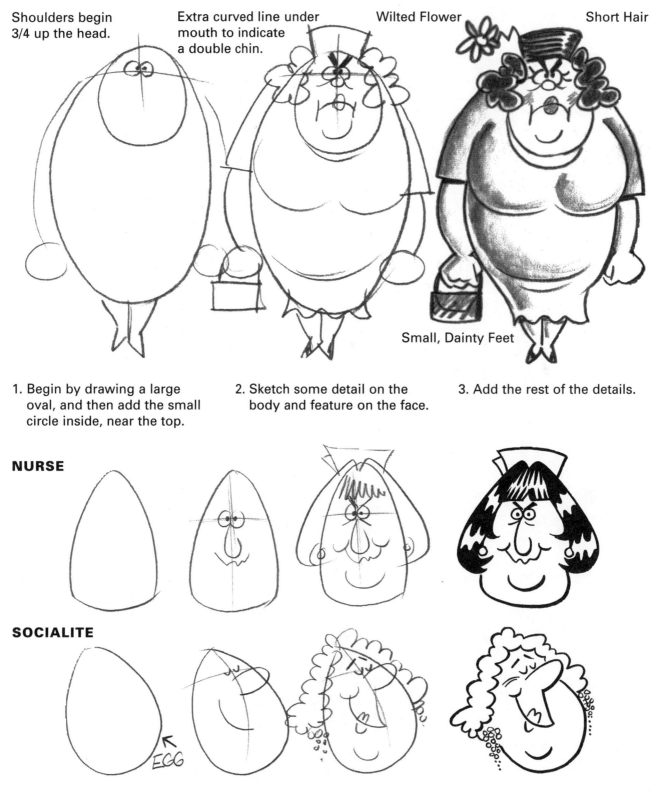

Shoulders begin
3/4 up the head.

Extra curved line under
mouth to indicate
a double chin.

Wilted Flower

Short Hair

Small, Dainty Feet

1. Begin by drawing a large
   oval, and then add the small
   circle inside, near the top.

2. Sketch some detail on the
   body and feature on the face.

3. Add the rest of the details.

NURSE

SOCIALITE

EGG

LINE OF ACTION!

Basic shape is a lima bean

This type works well in comical situations by being larger in relation to other characters, as with the nurse and patient below.

BORN TO SHOP

83

OLDER & LARGER MEN

This type could be used to convey either a friendly, "happy-go-lucky" feeling, or a feeling of intimidation. As with all characters, it depends on the situation and facial expression.

TOO ← MUCH PIZZA

A line divides the head from the body, leaving no neck.

1. Draw a large egg shape.

2. Wrap the guidelines around to make him face toward the right.

3. The legs taper to narrow ankles; the feet are drawn medium to large to give a feeling of balance.

IF YOU DARE... ...START WITH A PEAR!

MOVING MAN

When creating a character, it may help to associate the beginning shapes with recognizable objects.

BOWLER

GRANDPOP

HEAD OF BIG CORPORATION

PIZZA CHEF

TIMID & STUDIOUS TYPES

Draw this guy smaller and thinner than any other characters he appears with.

Variety is the thing you want to achieve when creating a cast of characters.

1. The head is as large as or larger than the torso.

2. Leave room for a large forehead (brains).

3. Add big glasses, neat hair, then legs, bow tie, and a sport jacket or suit. Also, the face tapers to a narrow chin.

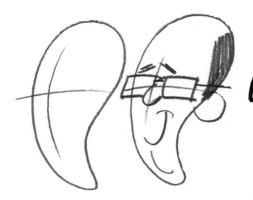

Sometimes it is best to leave out the eyes behind the glasses.

86

CREATE THE APPEARANCE OF MOTION.

1. Basic Construction.

2. Draw the character looking straight.

3. Add two more faces—one looking left and one looking right.

4. Draw a couple of sweeping circular lines around the three heads, and then add some lines, perspiration, and words. This step adds the movement.

BODY LANGUAGE

The facial expression is not the only thing that conveys emotion—often, the whole body has to be used to get your point across. It may be helpful to stand up—or sit down—and act out the action yourself; this way you can come up with the best pose for your drawing.

INANIMATE OBJECTS COMING TO LIFE!

(More on page 104)

BULLIES & BAD GUYS

You have to learn how to draw several different kinds of bad guys for your cartooning or you just won't have all the tools you need. Besides, this is your chance to get even!

1. Draw a large circle for the torso, and rough out short, squat legs.

2. Notice how the head seems to slump forward, making the shoulders appear larger.

3. An extreme haircut and a small forehead (lack of brains) add to the type (kid optional).

Lines on his face make him look like he needs a shave.

BASIC STANDING POSE

This is good because it gives a feeling of balance with the legs straddled and the feet pointing outward. By changing the arms and face you can use this standing pose for many situations.

Note the elements that make up this sinister guy: slicked-down hair, loud plaid sports jacket, straggly mustache, dark shade around the sides of his eyes, large toothy grin.

The contrast between the scoundrel and the sweet old lady is what makes this scene work so well.

"SOCK THE BULLY" MINI ANIMATION FEATURE

Lift Page Up & Down Here!

GLAMOROUS WOMEN

The glamorous woman is drawn basically the same as the "average" female, but with a few alterations.

LONG HAIR

LONG LASHES

COY EXPRESSION

SMALL WAIST

HOURGLASS FIGURE

LONG LEGS

REFINE FACIAL OUTLINE

MOTIVATIONAL TIP

Have a positive attitude!
Success comes in "Cans" . . .
Failure in "Can'ts."

"SOCK THE BULLY"
MINI ANIMATION
FEATURE

BABIES, KIDS & TEENS

These categories of cartoon characters can never be used up! Just look at all of the comic strips in your newspaper that feature babies, children, and teens. Note the subtleties that make a three-year-old look younger than an eight-year-old. It involves much more than making one taller than the other; you need to consider the proportion of body parts to each other.

Notice how the older characters have more prominent chins. . . .

Always keep a sketch pad handy; this way you can practice by quickly sketching kids at play.

| 0–1 YEARS | 3 YEARS | 5 YEARS | 8 YEARS | 14 YEARS | 16 YEARS |

BABIES

TEARDROP

NOTE - OLD FASHIONED WAY OF SUGGESTING A HIGHLIGHT OR SHINE". .TRY IT!

WAH·H!

Z·Z·Z·Z·Z

The cast shadow on this little guy's bathing suit and legs help to give this drawing a crisp look.

TODDLERS

Pretty cute, aren't they!

WHEELS ARE CYLINDERS

SCRE·E·E·E·E·E·E·E·E

LEAVE A GAP BETWEEN WHEELS & SHADOW ...IT LOOKS FASTER!!

Here is a way to add tone and shading to your art with the paper stump. (A paper stump is rolled-up paper that looks like a pencil, and is available in art stores.)

1. Using your HB pencil on the side of the point, make several strokes on a piece of paper.

2. Rub the tip of your paper stump over the pencil strokes.

3. Now use the stump to apply tone to your cartoon. This creates a soft, shaded look.

94

ANIMALS CAN MAKE YOUR CARTOONS FUNNIER!

SEZ WHO?!

TEENS

Drawing a character in a pose with his or her legs crossed may require the help of a model. Ask a friend or family member to pose for you. It can be a little tricky, but once you have the basic construction "roughed in," the rest is easy.

This fellow is strutting to the music! Notice that even though he is standing on one leg, he is still balanced.

SAME TEENAGER . . . DIFFERENT HAIRSTYLES!

To draw a prop like this car,
you must first break
it down to its basic elements
(cube and cylinders).
Sketch from photographs
of automobiles,
and simplify cartoon-style.

OLD AGE PAGE

Senior citizens are fun to draw, and they have interesting faces. They can spark ideas for numerous gags.

ONE TOOTH SHOWING

A FEW HAIRS

PRONOUNCED CHIN

BENT OVER

BONY LIMBS

RIDDLE What do you get from an overripe:

Prune

Squash

Zucchini

1.

2.

3.

BAH!

ANSWER A "MOLDY OLDY"

KEEP CONSTRUCTION OF THE WHEEL CHAIR SIMPLE...IT MAKES DRAWING THE CHARACTER ON IT, MUCH EASIER!

①

②

SPEED LIMIT 55

WHOOOOPEE-E-E

Note the cartoon effects that make these drawings work.

MONSTERS & CREEPY GUYS

Sometimes your art assignment calls for one of these . . . Yuck! . . . "whatevers!" They are fun to create because there are no rules—you can let your imagination run wild!

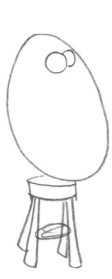

1. Begin with an egg shape.

2. Divide the egg in half horizon tally, and add some features.

3. Add as much detail and shading as you like: funny hat, sound effects, long eye lashes, spots on the body, etc.

THE MAD HIC-CUPPER!

Invent names for your creations based on what they do.

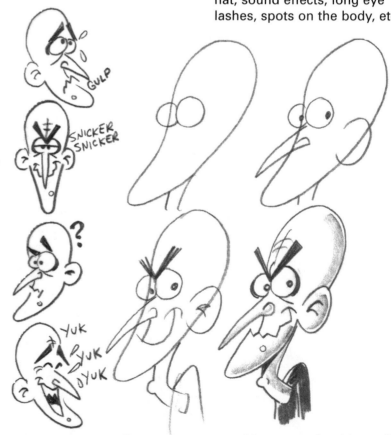

Can you come up with a name for this guy?

THE SILLIER YOU MAKE THEM, THE BETTER!

NOW LET'S CREATE A GENERALLY EVIL-LOOKING CHARACTER:

1. Draw a large oval for the body and an interesting shape for the head. By drawing the head lower than the line at the top of the oval, he appears to be stooped forward.

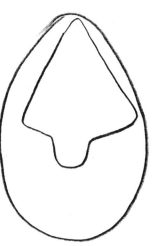

2. Give him a big smile with a lot of teeth, a large nose, and short legs.

3. Sketch in long arms that could almost touch the floor; then add a wild hairstyle, and direct the eyebrows downward for the sinister expression.

4. Now ink in the drawing; then erase the pencil lines. Notice the tint screen on the shirt. Tint screens, as we've discussed earlier, add a nice (or evil!) effect to a character.

MISCELLANEOUS TYPES

2 TRIANGLES
RECTANGLE

BAD COWBOY

SILLY TYPE

PUT FINGERS ON A CIRCLE FOR HANDS

SCIENTIST

KID BULLY

CARTOONIST

WOMAN BODYBUILDER

GAME-
SHOW
HOST

MOTIVATIONAL TIP

Be willing to take a chance.
You can't get to second base
with one foot still on first!

103

INANIMATE OBJECTS

Cartoon characters don't have to be human, you know! Adding human facial features to inanimate objects makes them come alive!

TELEVISION

WHAT'S ON TONIGHT?

VCR

LAMP & EASY CHAIR

IT'S EASY... TO DRAW AN EASY CHAIR!

DICTIONARY

DICTIONARY

MY LIPS ARE SEALED.. ..YOU CAN'T GET A WORD OUT OF ME!

First, look at the object and determine the best place to put the face. Also, you may find that there are parts of the object that can be easily adapted to hands, feet, hat . . . whatever! For example, the toothpaste coming out of the tube (below) is used for a ponytail.

BLENDER

Make up your own sound effects! (Spelling doesn't count.)

SPLOooSH!

PUT THE LID ON!

RRRRRRRRRR

ON

For gag ideas, think about what the object actually does. Chances are that there will be groundwork for many gags.

SCRUB-O TOOTHPASTE

TOOTHPASTE & TOOTHBRUSH

"Living" inanimate objects are great for advertising and animation.

SEWING MACHINE

A COOL JAZZ SAXOPHONE

ICE CREAM POPS

TOASTER & FRIEND

FOOD

CUTIE PIE

Try to create a "pleasing to the eye" design for your characters.

CLOTHES MAKE THE PERSON

Below we have some examples of how clothes help to define your character. There is special clothing associated with sporting events, occupations, and even time periods. Clothes can even have their own set of props and backgrounds.

By changing this man's neckwear, he can fit the part in all three roles:

BUTLER   **MAN OF THE CLOTH**   **JUDGE**

TOURIST

Dressing your character in the right clothes for the role he or she will be playing also requires the necessary props, such as the tourist's straw hat, camera, and shopping bag.

Here are some examples of specific uniforms associated with a character's work:

POLICEMAN

This man could also work as a delivery man, postal worker, or repairman by changing a few details.

WAITRESS

Notice she is wearing sensible shoes and holding an order pad and a pot of coffee (regular or decaf?).

DOCTOR

He could easily be adapted to be a pharmacist or a scientist, too.

EXERCISE

Look in the advertising section of your telephone book and practice drawing people with various types of clothing and props to fit the various listings. You'll really have to stretch your imagination for some of them!

KARATE EXPERT

HIPPIE FROM THE '60s

This elderly man could be cast as a wealthy banker, or even the mayor of the city. That is, as long as he is wearing his business suit . . . but look how easily he turns into a circus clown.

BANKER

CIRCUS CLOWN

REGIONAL APPAREL

Each country has its own set of costumes and props that establishes its culture. You may want to research the dress of people from foreign lands by looking through books and magazines at the library.

People from different parts of the same country have a distinct way of dressing, too.

FACIAL ACCESSORIES

These little extras help you to change the appearance of your characters and achieve variety. The characters in each row are actually the same character—look at what modifying a few external features can do!

1. Freckles and braids (you can draw freckles as circles, as shown here, or dots, as inexample #3).

2. Round glasses and a ponytail.

3. Freckles, hair down, and a headband.

4. Cat-eye glasses, curly hair, and a bow.

THESE TWO (NINE!) GUYS COULD BE INTERNATIONAL SPIES WITH ALL OF THESE DISGUISES.

PRACTICE BY MIXING AND MATCHING THESE ACCESSORIES ON DIFFERENT HEADS TO SEE HOW MANY COMBINATIONS ARE POSSIBLE. THIS TRICK COMES IN HANDY, ESPECIALLY FOR DRAWING DIFFERENT CHARACTERS FOR CROWD SCENES. BY THE WAY . . . CHECK OUT MY NEW SPECS!

HERE'S A FUN EXERCISE!

CHANGE DOUG'S MUG

TRACING PAPER

1. Draw a comic head without any eyebrows or hair on a piece of regular drawing paper.

2. Lay a piece of tracing paper over your drawing.

3. Now change Doug's "mug" without altering the original drawing. The possibilities are endless!

These are just a few examples!

FORM

Now that we have conquered the cartoon head and figure, the next thing to learn is how to draw where these characters will live! They will need to be surrounded by props and backgrounds. It's easy to do, and here's why:

ALL OBJECTS IN THIS WORLD (AND OTHER WORLDS) CAN BE DRAWN BY BREAKING THEM DOWN INTO ONE OR A COMBINATION OF THESE FOUR FORMS.

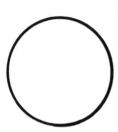  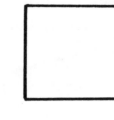 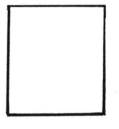

SPHERE   **CONE**   **CUBE**   **CYLINDER**

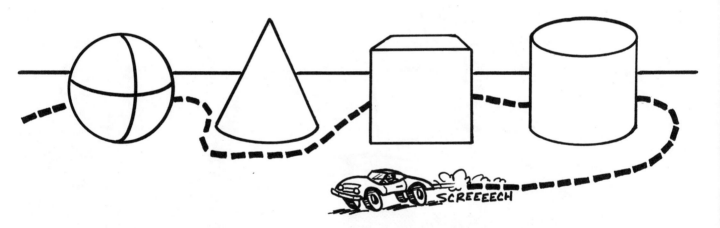

Form is the third-dimension. It gives the illusion of depth, as if you could actually go behind and in front of the object that you are drawing.

THE KEY IS TO SIMPLIFY

Develop the habit of seeing these four forms in everything you look at. It's your duty as a cartoonist. Somebody's got to do it!

You will find that although objects will break down into one or more of these basic forms, the resemblance may not be exact. For instance, a sphere may not be perfectly round and a cube may be long and tapered on one end, but they are still derived from the original forms.

CUBES

CYLINDERS

116

SPHERES

CONES

BY COMBINING THESE FORMS . . .
. . . YOU CAN DRAW ANYTHING.

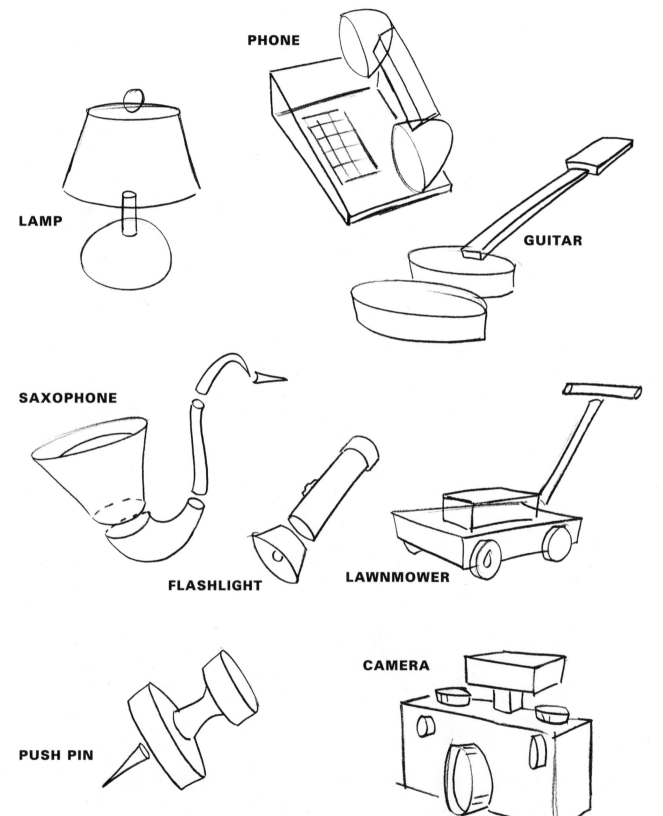

PHONE

LAMP

GUITAR

SAXOPHONE

FLASHLIGHT

LAWNMOWER

PUSH PIN

CAMERA

LIGHT, SHADE, AND CAST SHADOW

Now let's use what we've learned and take the next step—into light and shade. When you add these elements, your drawings will really jump right off the page. Simply put, shading will occur on the side of an object that is opposite the light source. As a rounded object moves toward the light, it will gradually get lighter. But light stops abruptly where flat planes meet, as in a cube.

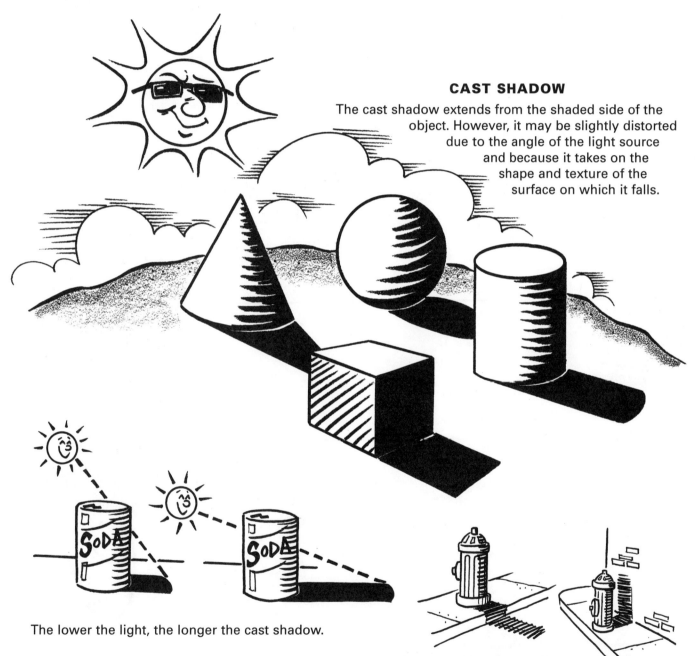

CAST SHADOW

The cast shadow extends from the shaded side of the object. However, it may be slightly distorted due to the angle of the light source and because it takes on the shape and texture of the surface on which it falls.

The lower the light, the longer the cast shadow.

The shadow follows the shape on which it falls.

Shading and cast shadows give your drawings a solid look. Remember, the first question to ask yourself is: "From which direction is the light coming?" Here are some "before and after" examples of objects with and without shading:

DESK

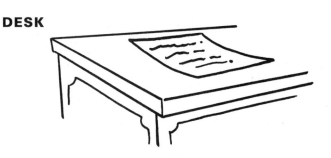

The cast shadow makes the paper appear more realistic.

SIGN

His lapels now have a three-dimensional look.

ROCKS

Shading done with lines looks best when they are evenly spaced and all drawn in the same direction.

So now when you stare at a blank piece of paper
and want to begin drawing, you will have a system!

1. Break objects down   2. Decide the direction   3. Shade accordingly.
   to their basic forms.   of the light source.

PROPS AND BACKGROUNDS

As the cartoonist, it's not only your job to cast the right characters for the parts and teach them to act, but you also have to select the appropriate backgrounds and correct props for them. These are important elements that help tell your story. For example, if you're telling a story about baseball, you need to suggest a stadium setting, a baseball glove, ball, bat, and so on. It's necessary for the reader to see these things, even though the props don't have to be drawn in great detail. In many cases, a few lines placed right will do the job nicely. The idea is to establish where the character is; and not to distract the reader. The goal is to simplify.

FAX MACHINE

This is all the reader needs to see in order to figure out that this is a fax machine.

MISCELLANEOUS PROPS AND THINGS

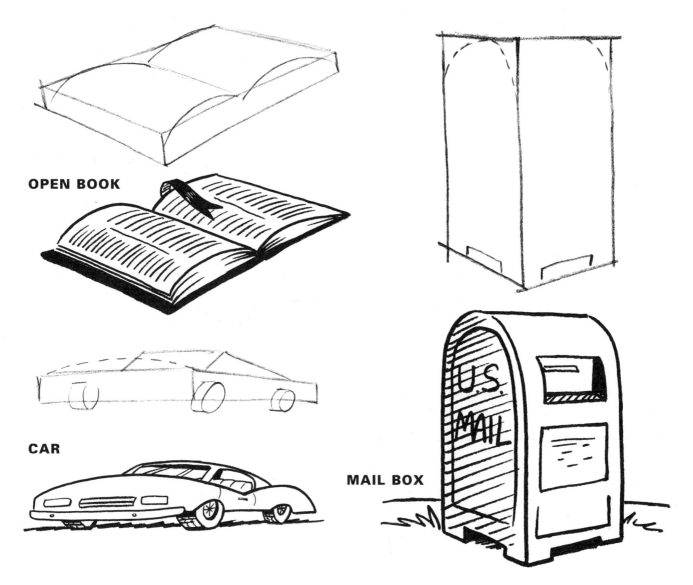

OPEN BOOK

CAR

MAIL BOX

JAN.

FEB.

MAR

APRIL

MAY

WINK

PRACTICE TIP #4

Draw Cartoons Everyday!

OK

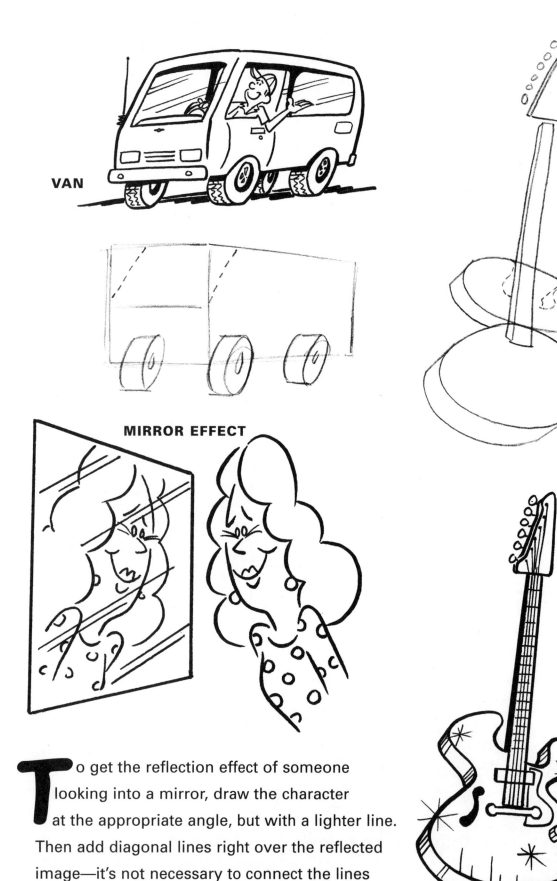

VAN

MIRROR EFFECT

ELECTRIC GUITAR

To get the reflection effect of someone looking into a mirror, draw the character at the appropriate angle, but with a lighter line. Then add diagonal lines right over the reflected image—it's not necessary to connect the lines of the reflected character to the frame of the mirror.

TREES

1. Lay a soft pencil on its side; while applying more pressure toward the point, draw a line for the trunk of the tree. This technique produces a sharp edge that softens gradually.

2. Next, use a sharp pencil to draw a line for the other side of the trunk, leaving some white space.

3. Make some looping lines for foliage, and add some texture to the bark (like some jagged lines and a knothole in the trunk).

4. Now add a cast shadow from all the leaves on the appropriate side.

ONE
Start with a cone shape.

TWO
Add squiggly lines for the branches.

TREE!
Shade the appropriate side.

TREES IN THE DISTANCE

Give very little detail to trees at middle distance. Indicate trees in the far distance simply, using up and down strokes with a felt tip pen.

MORE ENVIRONMENTAL PROPS

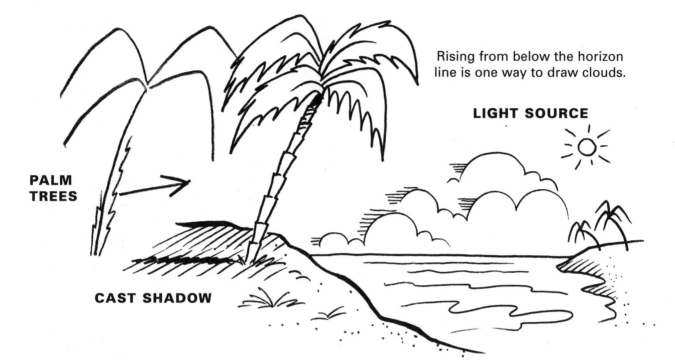

PALM TREES

CAST SHADOW

Rising from below the horizon line is one way to draw clouds.

LIGHT SOURCE

CLOUDS

Draw them fluffy and round, with a few lines indicating shading.

The water horizon line is straight, not squiggly, because it is way out in the distance.

RAIN CLOUDS

Draw more lines to make them appear darker and more ominous.

BOOM!

Drawing a face on this storm cloud adds an extra cartoon effect.

Drawing shading lines behind these clouds makes them seem to come to the foreground and stand out. Also remember that as the cloud gets further away, it will become smaller.

WATER EFFECTS

PUDDLES

Draw a free-form shape and add vertical lines to indicate a shiny effect.

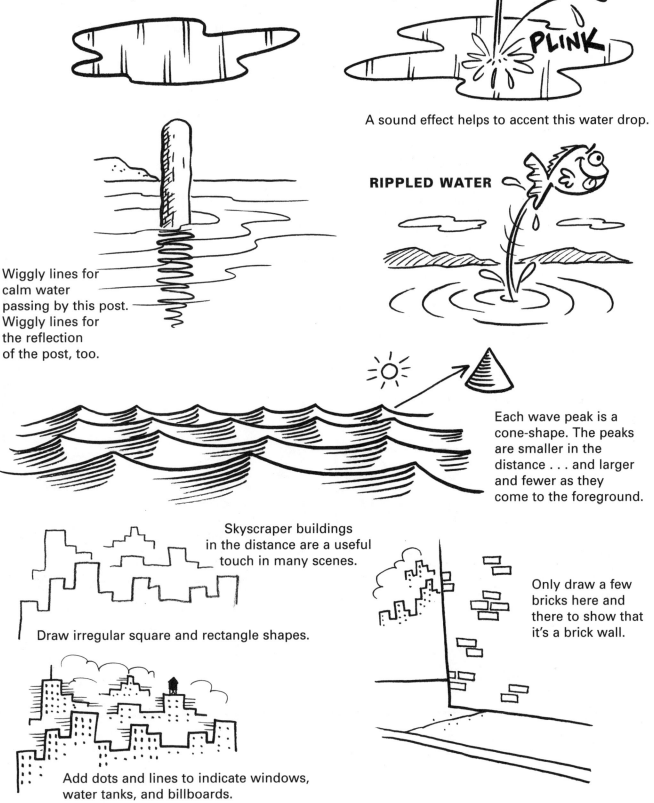

PLINK

A sound effect helps to accent this water drop.

Wiggly lines for calm water passing by this post. Wiggly lines for the reflection of the post, too.

RIPPLED WATER

Each wave peak is a cone-shape. The peaks are smaller in the distance . . . and larger and fewer as they come to the foreground.

Skyscraper buildings in the distance are a useful touch in many scenes.

Draw irregular square and rectangle shapes.

Only draw a few bricks here and there to show that it's a brick wall.

Add dots and lines to indicate windows, water tanks, and billboards.

127

PERSPECTIVE

Perspective is the process of drawing objects so they appear to have the correct depth or distance. Are you still there??? Hello! Don't get scared—it's easy to learn. And besides, we have only lost a few cartoonists so far by teaching perspective. So relax. All "perspective" really means is that objects seen further away seem smaller than when seen up close, even though they are really the same size. This is true of everything around you.

THREE THINGS TO KNOW

1. Viewpoint
2. Horizon Line
3. Vanishing Point

PERSON'S-EYE VIEWPOINT
Horizon line is in the middle.

WORM'S-EYE VIEWPOINT
Horizon line is low.

BIRD'S-EYE VIEWPOINT
Horizon line is high.

HORIZON LINE

This is where the sky meets the ground or water. This may not always be the same, because everything you draw is not outdoors. But try to determine where this horizon line would be drawn in relation to your view point: down low, average height, or very high, as shown in the previous sketches.

I UNDERSTAND HORIZON LINE AND VIEW POINT . . . BUT WHAT IS A VANISHING POINT?

IT'S THE POINT WHERE PARALLEL LINES COME TOGETHER, LIKE THE LINES FOR A ROAD OR RAILROAD TRACKS.

AH-HA! I GOTCHA! PARALLEL LINES NEVER COME TOGETHER. THAT'S WHY THEY'RE CALLED "PARALLEL LINES!"

TAKE IT EASY, MAN! I KNOW THAT. IT'S JUST THAT PARALLEL LINES ONLY SEEM TO COME TOGETHER AT THE VANISHING POINT . . . WHEN VIEWED IN PERSPECTIVE.

OH!

THERE ARE TWO TYPES OF PERSPECTIVE

ONE-POINT PERSPECTIVE

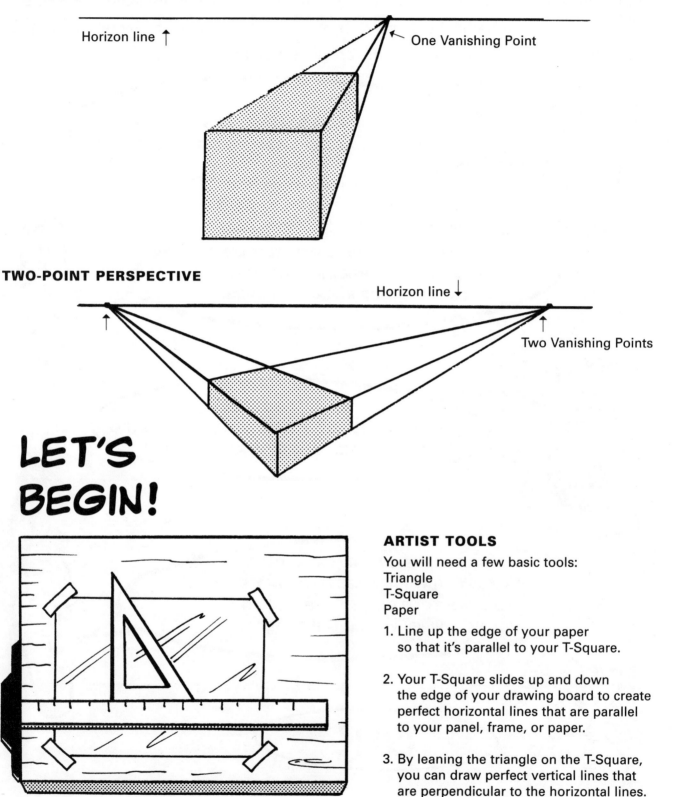

Horizon line ↑

One Vanishing Point

TWO-POINT PERSPECTIVE

Horizon line ↓

Two Vanishing Points

LET'S BEGIN!

ARTIST TOOLS

You will need a few basic tools:
Triangle
T-Square
Paper

1. Line up the edge of your paper so that it's parallel to your T-Square.

2. Your T-Square slides up and down the edge of your drawing board to create perfect horizontal lines that are parallel to your panel, frame, or paper.

3. By leaning the triangle on the T-Square, you can draw perfect vertical lines that are perpendicular to the horizontal lines.

ONE-POINT PERSPECTIVE

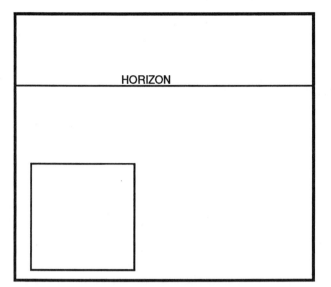

Draw a box and a horizon line. By drawing the horizon line above the box, it means we will see the top of the box.

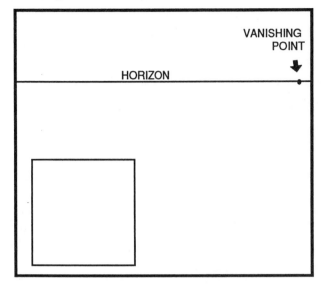

Draw the vanishing point on the horizon line. This is where the parallel sides will meet.

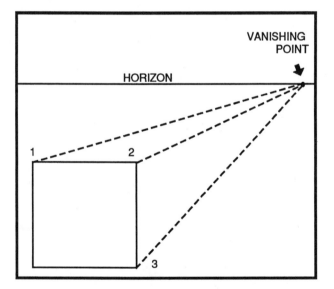

Draw lines from the three corners of the box to the vanishing point.

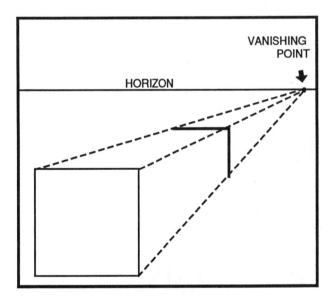

Next, draw a vertical and a horizontal line anywhere along these lines going to the vanishing point. It all depends on how deep you want your box to be.

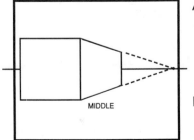

A. Here we have an example of where the horizon line is through the middle of the box, and only one side is seen in perspective.

B. In this case, the horizontal line is below the box, so you will see the bottom of the box.

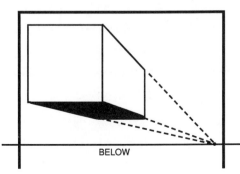

SOME EXAMPLES
OF ONE-POINT PERSPECTIVE

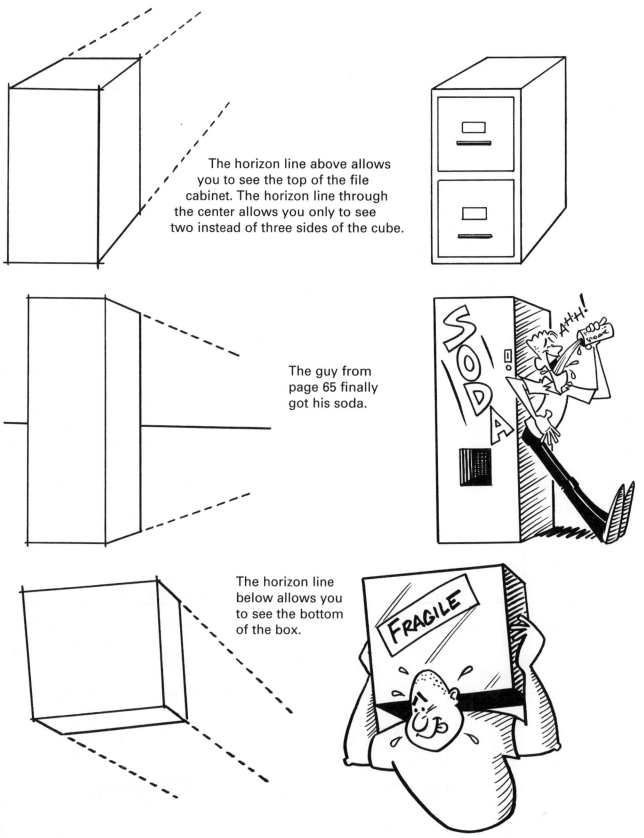

The horizon line above allows you to see the top of the file cabinet. The horizon line through the center allows you only to see two instead of three sides of the cube.

The guy from page 65 finally got his soda.

The horizon line below allows you to see the bottom of the box.

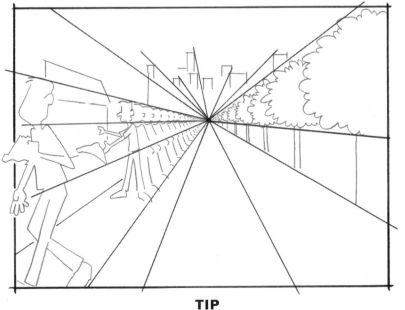

Looks like this guy is going to sell a lot of pizza. Everything in this picture that is seen in perspective meets at the same vanishing point, even the buildings. Notice how the figure eating pizza in the front of the frame is larger and in the correct size proportion to the guy buying pizza behind him. See how this continues down the (long) street. Also notice that the thickness of the line gets thinner as it goes into the distance.

133

TWO-POINT PERSPECTIVE

Two-point perspective has two vanishing points because the box
is turned enough so that two sides are seen in perspective.

Sides A and B (shaded) are
parallel, therefore they have
the same vanishing point.

Here sides C and D are parallel,
so they have the same vanishing point.

All other lines that make up the
sides of the box are vertical.

I ONLY SEE
TWO SIDES OF
THE BOX WHEN THE
HORIZON LINE IS
AT MY EYE LEVEL.

You can see under-
neath when the
horizon line is
below the box . . .
. . . and you can
see the top when
the horizon line
is above the box.

AN EXAMPLE OF TWO-POINT PERSPECTIVE

There could be a million objects in this scene. And although they all may have different vanishing points (the phone booth has different vanishing points than the buildings), they MUST use the same horizon line.

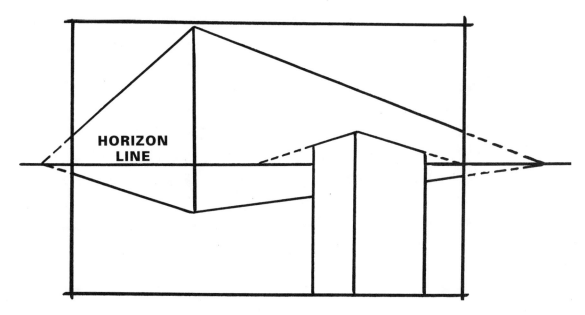

HORIZON
LINE

Watch out! Make sure the two vanishing points are not too close together in two-point perspective. It could make the object look odd or distorted.

To fix this, simply move the vanishing points further apart.

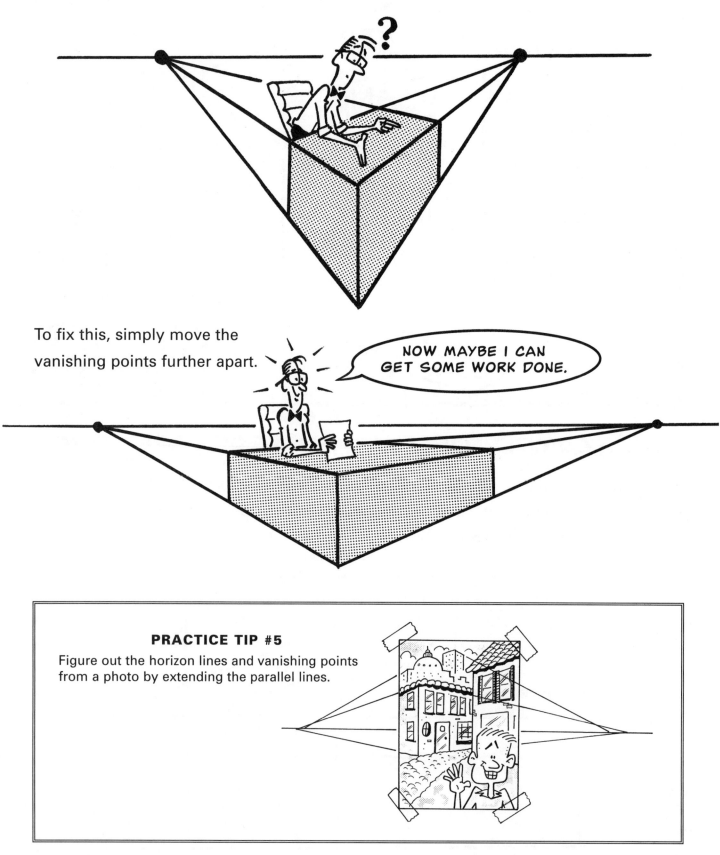

Some examples of how perspective comes in handy for us cartooners:

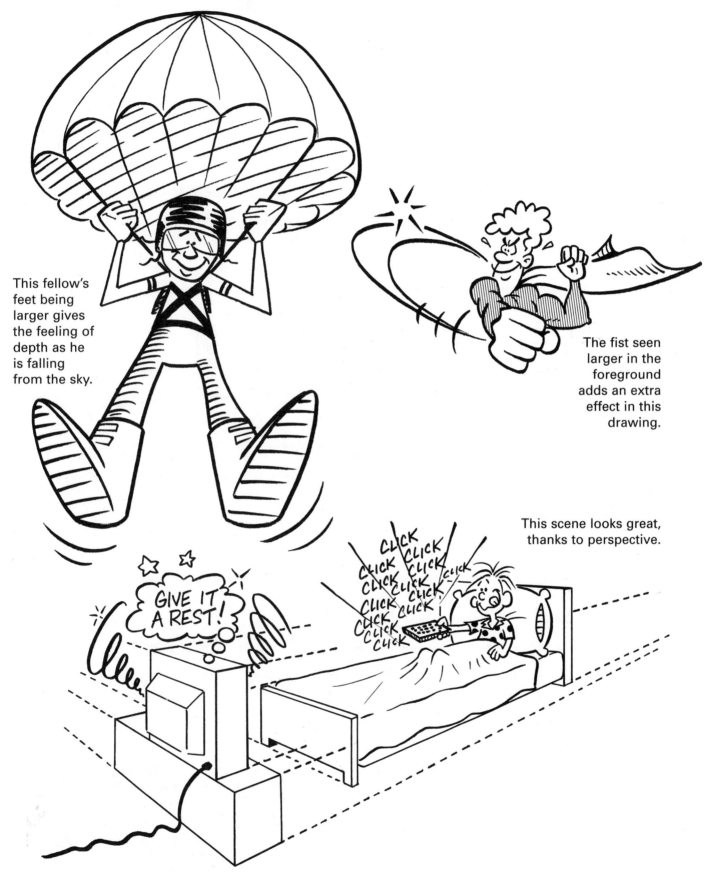

This fellow's feet being larger gives the feeling of depth as he is falling from the sky.

The fist seen larger in the foreground adds an extra effect in this drawing.

This scene looks great, thanks to perspective.

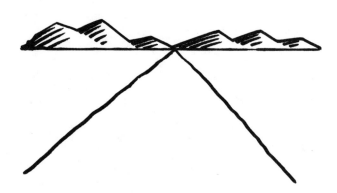

Just the same way that parallel lines are really the same distance apart . . .

. . . but seem to come together when seen in perspective . . .

. . . the same thing is true about posts or poles that are also evenly spaced . . .

. . . but appear to gradually get closer and closer in the distance when seen in perspective.

SO HOW DO I FIGURE OUT HOW TO SPACE THEM CORRECTLY IN PERSPECTIVE?

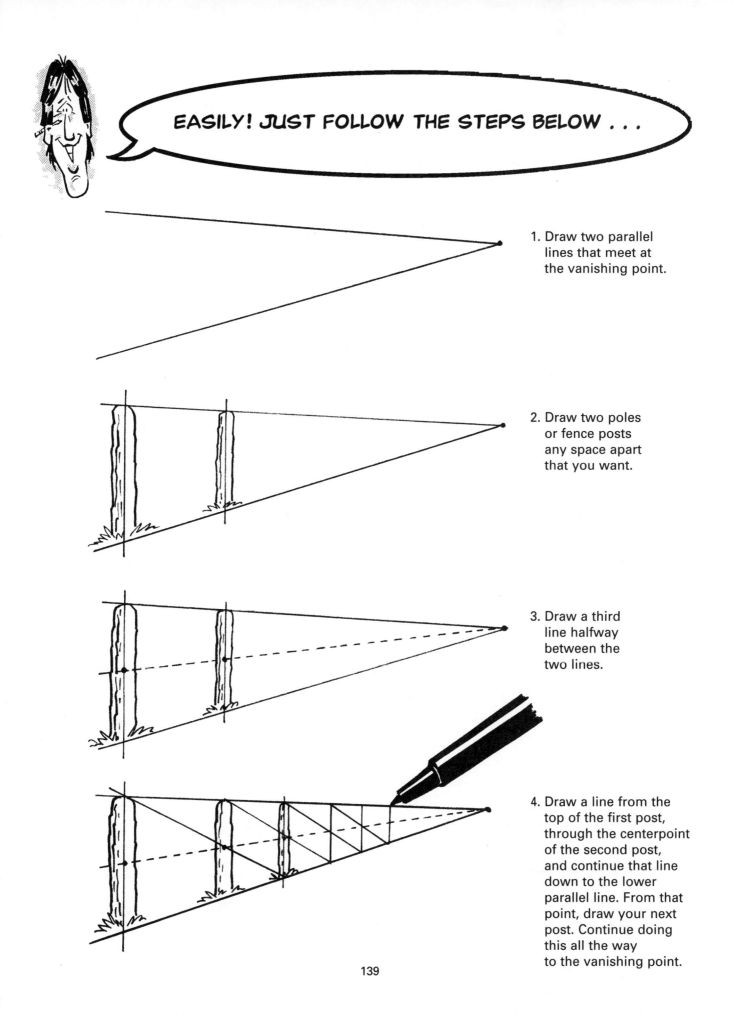

EASILY! JUST FOLLOW THE STEPS BELOW . . .

1. Draw two parallel lines that meet at the vanishing point.

2. Draw two poles or fence posts any space apart that you want.

3. Draw a third line halfway between the two lines.

4. Draw a line from the top of the first post, through the centerpoint of the second post, and continue that line down to the lower parallel line. From that point, draw your next post. Continue doing this all the way to the vanishing point.

BACKGROUNDS

Afew well-placed props, along with your basic knowledge of perspective, is all you need to establish a setting for your character. Be careful not to put too much detail into the props because you want the main character(s) to stand out. Remember to draw just enough props to let the reader know where the character is—and stop there. Keep it simple, and refer to your art morgue for ideas.

LABORATORY OR PHARMACY

In this top drawing, the bottles behind her have been drawn with a thick line and there are many more than in the drawing below. This drawing works okay, but not as well as the one below where the bottles have been drawn with a thinner line and with spaces between. The reader still gets the idea of a laboratory or pharmacy setting, but is not distracted from the main character. Also notice how only one beaker is filled-in in the bottom drawing, so as not to take the eye away from the main action of the drawing.

LIVING ROOM

Notice how I have stopped drawing the books and shelf where his head is. Also notice that the character is not placed in the center of the rectangle, but instead is placed a little off to the right, allowing for a better composition.

SNOW SCENE

This background is a very simple one to do. Try not to fill in the props and background—this allows it to look more like snow. After the drawing is done, I simply make a lot of circles over everything for snowflakes, and lines for their direction.

STADIUM

The grandstand behind the players is all that is needed to indicate this stadium setting. This could easily work for football, soccer, tennis, or any other sporting event.

Here we have a bank setting drawn from two angles. The first one shows the action from the customer's point of view, and the other looking over the shoulder of the teller at the customer. The best one to use depends on which tells your story better.

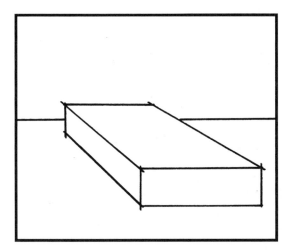

Look how many background settings we can get from this one cube by changing a few details.

POOL HALL

OFFICE

BEDROOM OR HOSPITAL ROOM

BATHROOM

TO DRAW CARTOON ANIMALS, THE KEY IS TO SIMPLIFY!

Realistic

"Cartoonified"

IT MUST BE TOUGH FOR THIS CAT TO MAKE UP HIS MIND!

TIP: Use photographs of your own pet or pictures from your art morgue as guides to practice drawing your own cartoon animals.

ry to BEAR with me on this! By using the realistic bear on the upper left as a guide, we can create cartoon bears. For example, we can see that he has a squarish nose, a friendly smile, a lot of fur, and ears on top of his head. So, simply transfer these features into one definite, black, cartoon-style line . . . and there it is!

HERE IS AN EASY WAY TO DRAW "A" BEAR.

1.   2.   3.   4.

Turning this letter into a bear is called a "doodle trick."
There are lots more fun-to-do tricks like this later in the book!

APES BEGIN WITH SHAPES

1. Use pencil to loosely draw a shape for the head. Now *there* is something to build on!

2. Now add the features. For an ape, keep the eyes high and the mouth low. This step is where you should make all your corrections.

3. If you are satisfied with everything, go ahead and ink it in with marker or pen and ink. Wait a few moments for the ink to dry, then erase the pencil lines. There's your finished drawing!

THE HEAD AND THE BODY ARE PEAR SHAPES

To change a male ape into a female ape like this lovely creature, begin with the same basic shape and features, then add a few extra touches, such as lipstick, a flower in the hair, curls, earrings, eyelashes, etc. If this were in color, I'd add some extra red to her cheeks, too. Be creative—make your cartoons funny!

CARTOON EFFECTS AND ACCESSORIES WORK GREAT WITH ANIMALS, TOO!

Don't overdo the background—you want the main character to stand out.

1. Rough out shapes for the head and the body. Use double lines to show the thickness of the arms and legs. (Notice how much longer the arms are than the legs.) Experiment with the positioning of the ape until you are satisfied.

2. Now add the facial expression to communicate the idea of the sketch. Remember, the definition of a cartoon is "a drawing that expresses a funny idea." You can also begin to develop the drawing with props.

3. Continue refining the sketch; make changes as you go.

4. Now go over the drawing with a marker. I used one with a thick point and made loose up-and-down strokes. You can't go wrong when drawing fur like this—it always looks good! But try to leave some white space for highlights.

EXPERIMENT WITH SHAPES TO MAKE YOUR CARTOONS LOOK DIFFERENT. THAT'S THE MON KEY!

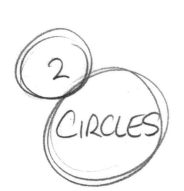  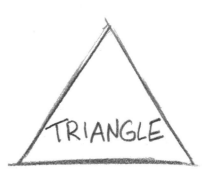

PRACTICE TIP #6

Sketch animals at the zoo!

CRUNCH

CHOMP CHOMP CHOMP

MONKEY

HORSES

Horses are fun to draw and they come in handy for
adding movement and action to your drawings!

Notice how the horse to the
right is running—with its hind
legs forward and its front legs
back. Horses don't really run
this way, but this is "cartoon
world" and if you think that it
works better for the drawing . . .
DO IT!

Also, notice the cartoon effects
and accessories that were
added to show speed.

DANGER!
CLIFF CLOP
CLOP

PANT
PANT

TROT
TROT
TROT

DON'T
FORGET TO ADD
SOUND EFFECTS . . .
THEY'LL MAKE YOUR
CARTOONS FUNNIER!

THERE ARE MANY DIFFERENT WAYS TO DRAW HORSES!

←OVALS

ORDINARY HORSE

RACE HORSE

LADY HORSE

B-zzzz

B-zzz

LOOKS LIKE HE NEEDS A SHAVE!

Make the ears a little longer and he's a Mule!

Draw stripes to turn him into a Zebra!

BODY PROPORTIONS

The degree to which you distort these proportions depends on your style of cartooning. Sometimes it's fun to take them to the "max!"

THE SILLIER THE BETTER!

The sketch above was done with a fine point marker.

DOGS

Friends to everyone . . . especially a cartoonist!

Notice how they are built from a combination of shapes.

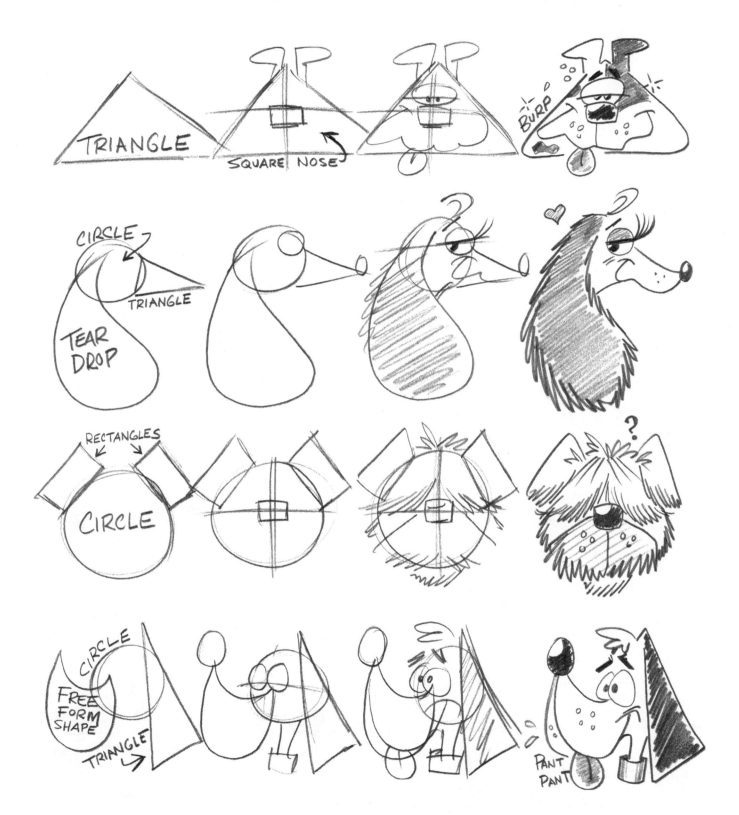

DOG BODIES

Dogs come in
all shapes and sizes.
Some are hairy,
and some aren't.
Change the expression to
change the personality.

Cartoon dogs can walk upright like humans, or they can be down on all fours, as shown below.

The shadow directly under the dog's feet makes him appear to be walking slowly.

But drawing the shadow slightly below the feet with a few speed lines makes him appear to be running . . . and the dogs are the same drawing!

Basic Four-legged Walking Pose
Here the front legs are in the opposite position of the back legs and it works well; however, you can draw them in any combination you think looks good.

SEE HOW THEY RUN!

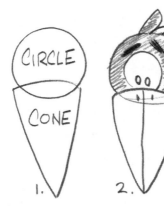
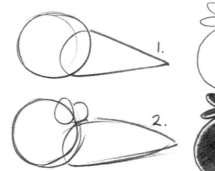

The best thing about cartoon birds is that you can draw them any way you wish and it always works! This is done by modifying the size and shape of the beak, neck, and body, and by creating funny bird feet.

TURN FEATHERS INTO HANDS

THE LINE INSIDE THE BEAK AND THE EYES, DETERMINE THE **EXPRESSION!**

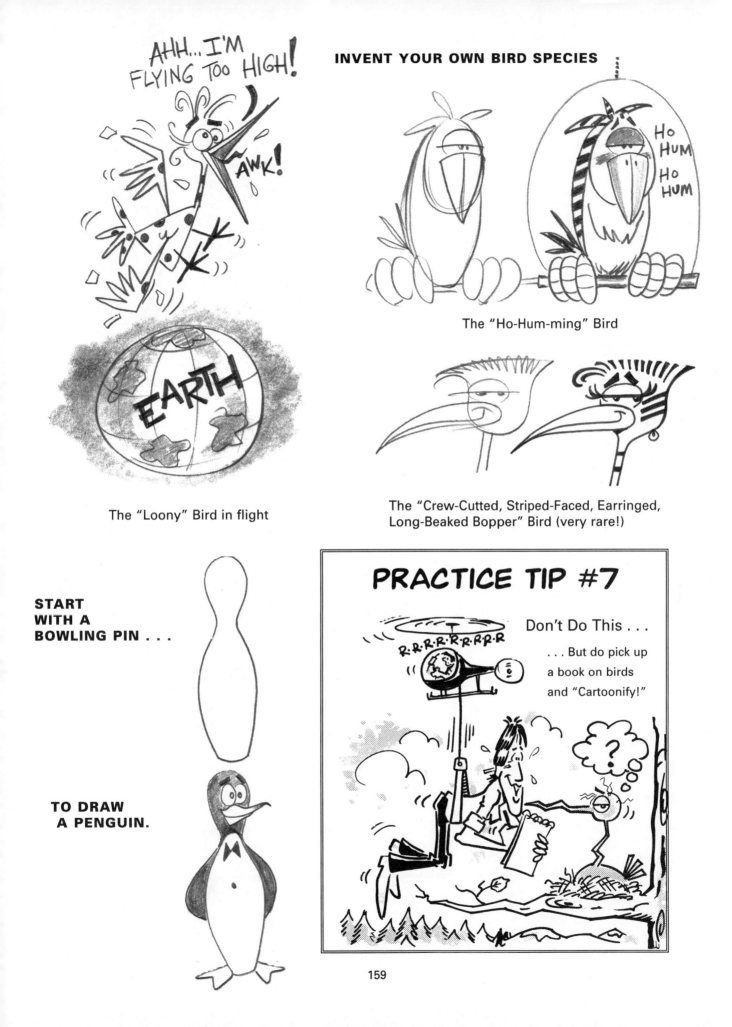

INVENT YOUR OWN BIRD SPECIES

The "Ho-Hum-ming" Bird

The "Loony" Bird in flight

The "Crew-Cutted, Striped-Faced, Earringed, Long-Beaked Bopper" Bird (very rare!)

START WITH A BOWLING PIN . . .

TO DRAW A PENGUIN.

PRACTICE TIP #7

Don't Do This . . .

. . . But do pick up a book on birds and "Cartoonify!"

159

AL OWL

OPRAH OSTRICH

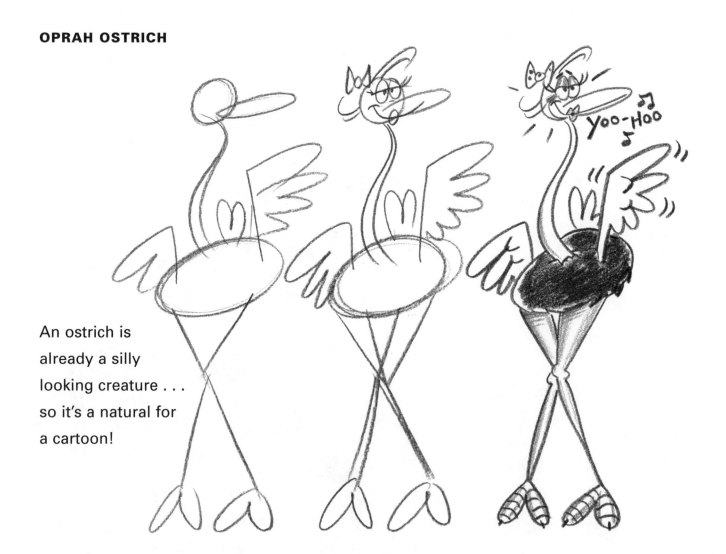

An ostrich is
already a silly
looking creature . . .
so it's a natural for
a cartoon!

ELEPHANTS

Two simple shapes are the basic elements for drawing these portly creatures.

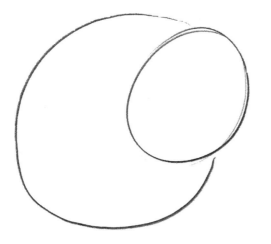

EYES ARE LOW ON HIS HEAD. MAKES HIM CUTER!

1. Draw a large circle for the body and a smaller one for the head.

2. Now add two guidelines for the features. Think of his head as a three-dimensional object and wrap the guidelines around it. Also, add stumpy legs.

BLACK

SHORT TAIL

3. Continue to refine the drawing; when you are satisfied, begin inking.

4. Draw lines on the trunk to give the impression of creases. Also, don't forget the curlicues for the knees!

Modify the beginning shapes to create this large female elephant. Notice that the legs were drawn a bit thinner towards the top. This makes her appear taller. The added touches, such as the tutu, the crown, and the ribbon turn her into a circus elephant.

TRUNKS
ARE
FUN.

. . . AND
<u>HAND</u>—Y!

TA-DA-A!

I THINK
I SNEEZED
TOO HARD
THAT TIME!

The end of the trunk can become a hand, if needed.

WOOOSH

Notice the eyes on this one. This is "Old Style" cartooning . . . but it's always in style with me! Try it!

162

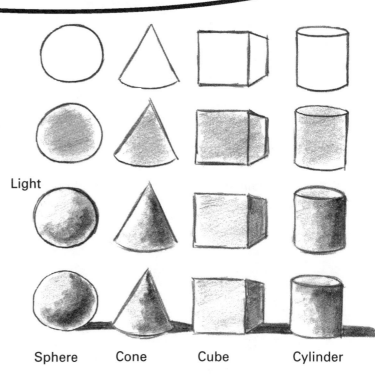

LET'S RECAP THE PRINCIPLES OF FORM AND SHADING. REMEMBER . . . THEY ADD THE POWER OF THE THIRD DIMENSION TO YOUR DRAWINGS! (SEE HOW IT HELPS THE BEACH ELEPHANT BELOW.)

FORM—These four basic forms are used in various combinations to create just about anything!

TONE—Tone is the overall color of the object. In this case, we are working in black and white, so the tone will be gray.

SHADING—Shading adds depth. Decide from which direction the light is coming, then shade the opposite side.

CAST SHADOW—The cast shadow extends from the shaded side and takes on the shape of the object—slightly distorted.

Light

Sphere   Cone   Cube   Cylinder

Let's Apply These Principles to this "Elephant at the Beach" Scene

This bathing beauty was made from the four basic forms shown above. Notice, however, that the shapes are modified a bit and they are not exact. The head and body are spheres, the legs and trunk are cylinders, the hat is a cone, and the cooler is a cube.

TIP: Use a paper stump for blending and softening tones.

LIONS

Now for the "king of beasts!" Let's begin this one with a diamond shape, then add a few simple shapes to it.

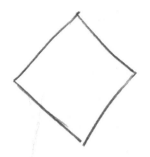  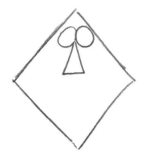

1. Draw an ordinary diamond shape.

2. Add two circles for the eyes and an elongated triangle for the nose.

3. Draw the pupils; leave some white for the highlight. Add an upside-down triangle to complete the nose.

4. Start from the point of the nose and draw two squiggly lines for the mouth, as shown. Also, draw two circles for the ears.

5. Add details such as small circles and lines for the whiskers and the beard.

6. Now for the mane! Use your entire wrist for drawing the loose, curved strokes.

BODY
The body is a teardrop shape. Build on this shape by adding the legs and the tail, then shade accordingly. Notice all the diagonal lines that were used to shade the two legs farthest from the viewer's eye. This creates a different shading effect which is good for adding variety.

Here are more beginning shapes that work well:

FILLED IN OVALS FOR EYES.

"STYLIZED MANE FOR VARIETY

2 CIRCLES FOR THIS SIDE VIEW

PLAIN OLD CIRCLE

GLASSES (WHY NOT?)

NOSE IS ALSO A TRIANGLE FROM THE SIDE

Start with a Heart!

1.

2.

3.

4.

STANDING UPRIGHT

Change his paws to hands, make big feet, and don't forget the crown (a little respect please!).

165

ANIMALS LOOK LIKE PEOPLE . . . OR IS IT THE OTHER WAY AROUND?

Whatever . . . but as you can see, it is definitely true!

As a cartoonist, it is important to develop the habit of observing people constantly—this will improve your drawing skills.

FISH

MUTT

The key to drawing these animal/people lookalikes is to have their features simulate the same shapes. For example, the black noses on the mutt and the bulldog pictured here are the same shapes as their respective lookalike human's noses. Also, you can substitute long hair for long ears. Body proportions can also be drawn to resemble each other. This is a great way to "squeeze out" an extra bit of humor.

BULLDOG

COCKER SPANIEL

FROG

GOAT

MONKEY

PARROT

BARNYARD ANIMALS

COW

1. Begin with a bunch of shapes. It's fun and helpful to compare the shape of the object you are drawing to something else, such as the kidney shape shown here.

2. Refine the sketch by adding facial features, thickness to the legs, and a bell around the neck.

3. Knowing that the light is coming from the upper right, begin to add the shading.

4. Use a paper stump or lay the pencil on its side and lightly blend the tones. Add a few effects & accessories such as motion lines by the tail and "shine lines" around her contented face!

LAMB

CHICKEN

PIG

It is important to study the features of animals. For example, noses vary from one animal to another, as do ears. Also, the little extras like beards, horns, and antlers are critical points of likeness. Once you are familiar with what it takes to draw a particular creature, you can then draw it from any angle and with any facial expression.

HEAVY BLACK LINE AROUND HIS EYES MAKES HIM LOOK.. ANGRY!

MUNCH MUNCH

THEY WILL EAT ANYTHING!

PRACTICE TIP #8

Always be thinking of funny situations for your cartoon animals to be in.

SNORT

MISCELLANEOUS ANIMALS

KANGAROO

JUST DRAW A SMALLER VERSION

SEAL   **BULL**   **RABBIT**   **MOUSE**

1.

2.

3.

LOOKS ALRIGHT... ..OK WITH ME... ..YES I'LL GO ALONG WITH THAT...IT'S FINE WITH ME...

"THE SEAL OF APPROVAL"

RIDDLE

What do these three objects have in common?

FOOTBALL   BELL   ONION

DING DONG

ANSWER

Nothing . . . except that they are all great beginning shapes for drawing a cat!

INSECTS
& OTHER CRAWLING THINGS

...ARE ANIMALS TOO

MOSQUITO

SPIDER

BUTTERFLY

CATERPILLAR

Why not make up your own bugs? That's what cartooning is all about! Also, it doesn't matter what kind of features you draw on your bugs because nobody really knows what they're supposed to look like anyway. So have fun with them!

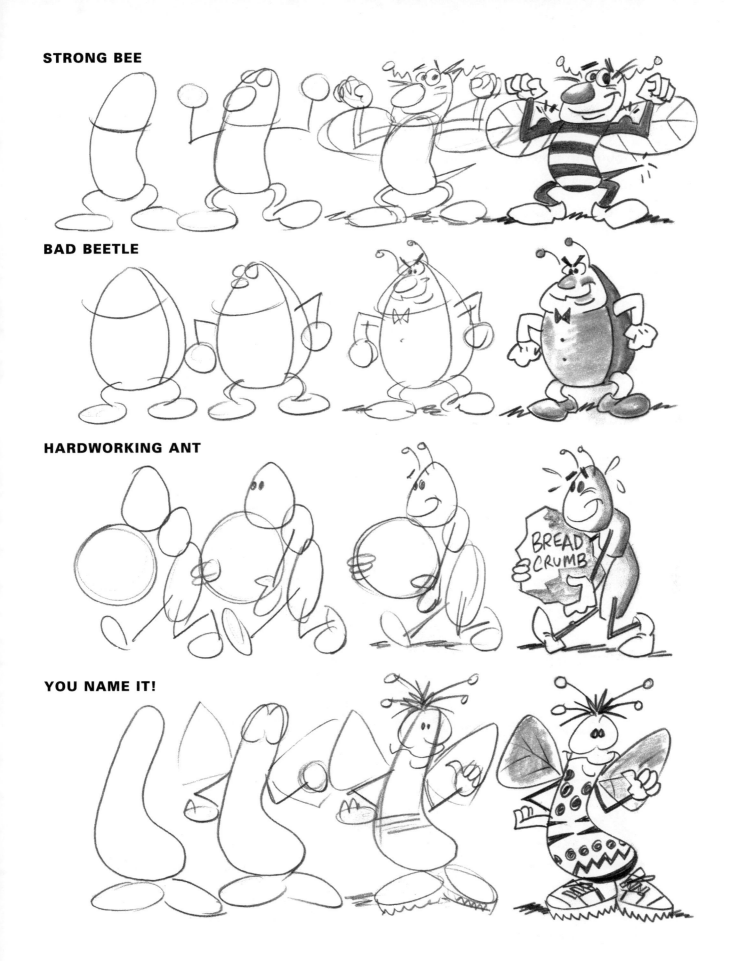

STRONG BEE

BAD BEETLE

HARDWORKING ANT

BREAD
CRUMB

YOU NAME IT!

173

DINOSAURS

Dinosaurs are fascinating! They come in many different shapes and sizes which makes them perfect for cartooning. They often turn up in movies in both realistic and cartoon forms. The best way to continue your study of these spectacular creatures is to get a book on dinosaurs and sketch away.

To draw the "king of the dinosaurs," simplify his massive body to somewhat of an egg shape and make his head squarish. He has a thick tail which tapers to a point and very short, muscular arms.

TYRANNOSAURUS REX

Now draw the facial features—give him very sharp teeth because this is what he is known for. Add some scales, spots, and shading to his body to make him look solid, then draw the cast shadow. Scary, isn't he!

TAPER THE NECK

HANDS

SHORT MUSCULAR ARMS

1.

2.

3.

STEGOSAURUS

SKINNY EGG SHAPE

FRONT VIEW

This guy looks narrow from the front. I have drawn him to look friendly . . . and who knows? Maybe he was! You can have fun drawing the tail curling in different ways, and by the way, check out those toenails!

LEGS GET WIDER AT THE BOTTOM

HE LOOKS HAPPY!

WE'RE MAKIN'.. HISTORY-Y-Y-Y!

"WATCH HIM WINK" Mini-Animation FEATURE

Lift Page Up & Down Here!

UNDERWATER CREATURES

Cartoon fish are a lot like cartoon birds and insects because you can make up your own species. The sky's . . . uh . . . I mean, the sea's the limit!

FISH

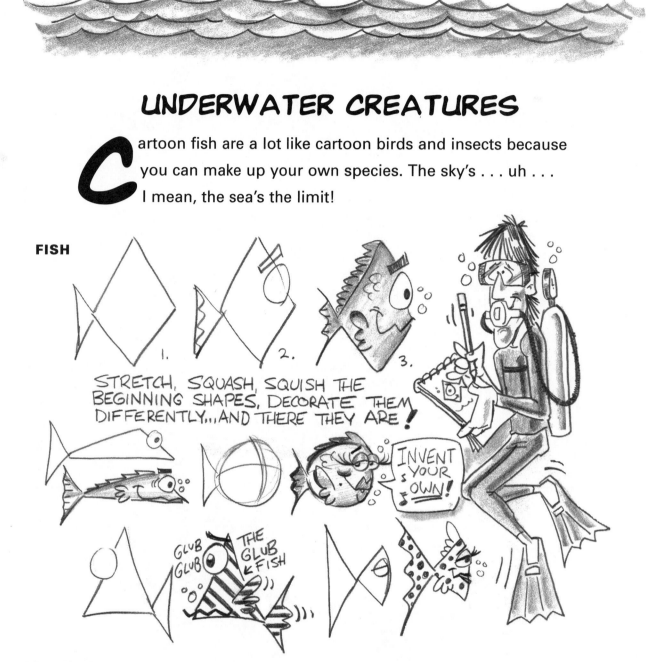

STRETCH, SQUASH, SQUISH THE BEGINNING SHAPES, DECORATE THEM DIFFERENTLY...AND THERE THEY ARE!

INVENT YOUR OWN!

GLUB GLUB THE GLUB FISH

GIANT CLAM

1. Start with a simple oval. Then divide it in half with a squiggly line.

2. Next, add two large eyes, eyebrows, and a tongue (because he probably just ate a poor, unfortunate fish), then refine the oval a little more. Don't forget the bubbles!

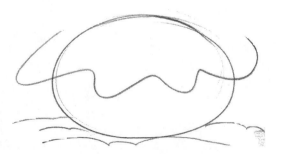

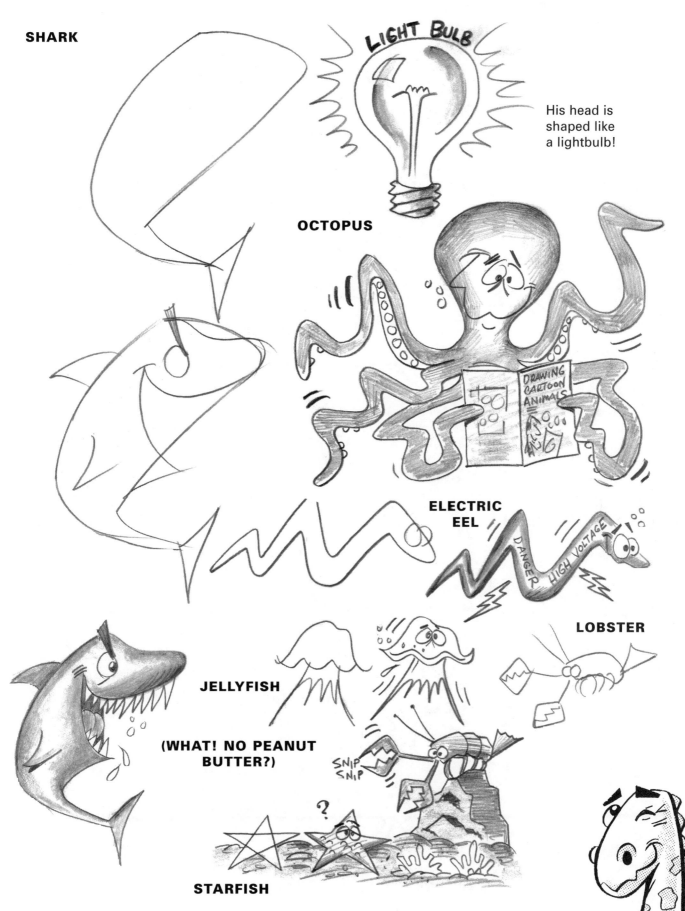

SHARK

LIGHT BULB

His head is shaped like a lightbulb!

OCTOPUS

ELECTRIC EEL

DANGER HIGH VOLTAGE

DRAWING CARTOON ANIMALS

LOBSTER

JELLYFISH

(WHAT! NO PEANUT BUTTER?)

SNIP SNIP

?

STARFISH

177

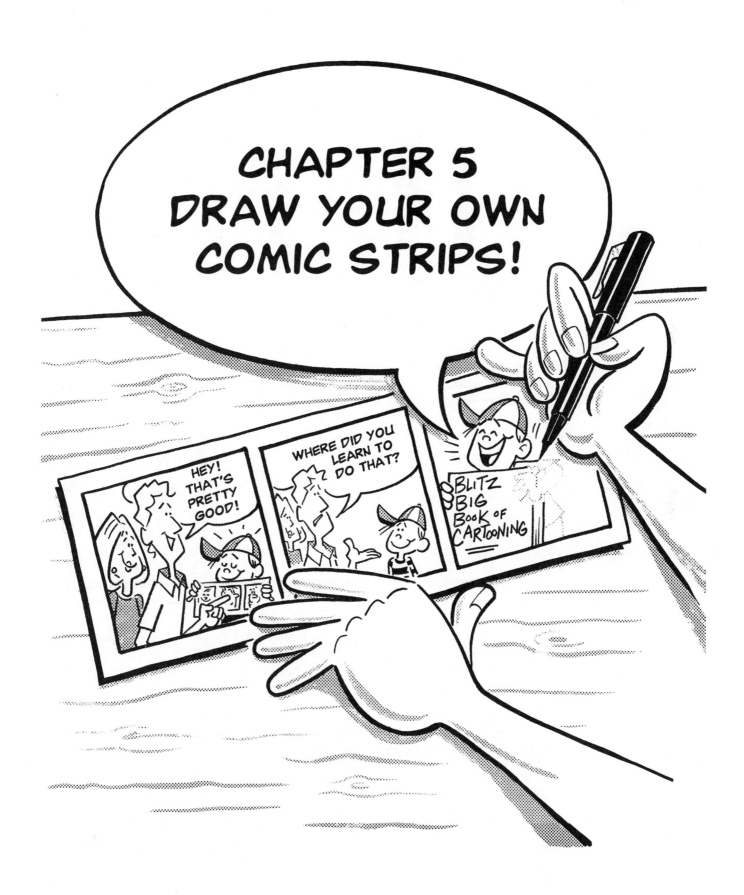

Have you ever noticed how may people clip comic strips out of the newspaper and display them next to their desks, or on their refrigerators, or next to their station in the bank? Have you seen them taped on the cash register at a store or pinned up on the bulletin board at work?

This is because comic strips deal with real-life things that we can all identify with. They really hit home by making fun of our daily troubles and by reminding us not to take ourselves too seriously.

As a cartoonist, you can have a lot of fun creating your own comic strip. You design the characters, make up the world in which they live, invent funny situations, and give them the words to say. . . . Then you get to watch people enjoy what you have done! Drawing a comic strip is a great way to get your story told!

Sooner or later, almost everyone who likes to draw cartoons tries to do a comic strip. This chapter will give you some idea of how to go about it.

THE ANATOMY OF A COMIC STRIP

A. PANELS
(cartoon blocks)

B. BORDERS
(lines around panels)

C. TALK BALLOONS

D. THOUGHT BALLOONS

E. POINTERS
(shows who is speaking)

F. BOLD WORD
(used for emphasis)

G. EFFECTS & ACCESSORIES
(help tell the story)

A STRIP IS BORN!
OR . . . THE PROCESS AT A GLANCE

1. HAVE THE IDEA!

2. JOT DOWN THE IDEA
(Anywhere you can . . . before you forget!)

3. DESIGN THE CAST OF CHARACTERS

4. ROUGH IT OUT
Dialog writing & gag setup

5. CUT PAPER TO SIZE

6. PENCIL IN
- Borders
- Lettering
- Cartooning

7. INK IN
- Borders
- Lettering
- Cartooning

8. ERASE PENCIL & FILL IN LARGE BLACK AREAS

9. WATCH PEOPLE ENJOY WHAT YOU HAVE DONE!

IDEAS & GAGS

The main ingredient of a comic strip is the gag (or joke). Without it, there would be no reason to draw! But can you imagine coming up with a new gag everyday? Well, that is exactly what you must do if you sell your feature to a newspaper. But do not fear! With this book you will learn many ways to stimulate ideas.

REGULAR CHARACTERS—Ideas can be sparked simply by picking out certain aspects of your characters and highlighting or exaggerating them—personality quirks, physical traits, or the environmental conditions in which they live. Look at other comic strips and notice how each character has at least one recognizable trait that belongs to him or her alone.

You must know your character thoroughly so you can focus your writing on things that you know he or she would or wouldn't do. For example, if the character is a little boy who is always being pursued by a little girl, you can build jokes around that situation. Or, why not create a dog who loves to eat pizza? Once your characters' personalities are established, you can place them in the same everyday situations your readers might face.

ADDING CHARACTERS—Sometimes you will come up with an idea for a joke that does not fit your main character's personality, but it's too good to discard. Don't try to force it on the main character—simply create another one, apply the joke, and add this new character to the strip. (This is how you build your supporting cast.)

You may choose to write comic strips or single panel cartoons that do not have a regular cast of characters. These can be seen daily in the newspaper or magazines. The humor in these features can be totally unrelated from day to day. You may find this a less restrictive way of writing gags.

MAKING UP JOKES

Because humor is a very personal thing, each person must find his or her own method of making up funny gags. Sometimes jokes come to mind quickly; other times they do not come as quickly (and maybe not at all!). However, once you develop your own technique and a habit for "thinking funny," you will be amazed at how many jokes pop into your head throughout the day. You may find (happily) that you will not be able to stop them!

Here are some ways to get started:

1. DOODLING—General sketching will sometimes stimulate an idea for a gag.

2. LOOKING AT OTHER STRIPS—Check out strips in a current newspaper or go to the library where you can look at old comic strips on microfilm. Make up original jokes based on established concepts of humor.

For example:

SIGHT GAG (WORDLESS)
ELEMENT OF SURPRISE
REVERSE SITUATION
PLAY ON WORDS
STUPIDITY
CLICHÉ

3. THINKING TOPICAL—Look in magazines, watch television, go to movies, read the newspaper, and listen to the radio. Make a list of what is "hot" at the moment, such as clothing styles, computers, politics, etc. Chances are you will find that a lot of humor can be squeezed out of something that everyone is talking about.

4. THE CALENDAR—Look through a calendar and write down all the events associated with a particular month or time of year. You will be surprised at how long the list will be. Each event has its own built-in set of props, cast of characters, and unique circumstances. Study these and you'll find inspiration for many gags.

Here are just a few:

GIFT-GIVING   THANKSGIVING

SUNBURNS   VACATION   TAXES

PROMS   SPRING CLEANING

RAKING LEAVES   FOOTBALL SEASON   GROUNDHOG DAY

ST. PATRICK'S DAY

BACK-TO-SCHOOL   HAY FEVER

BARBECUES   FATHER'S DAY

REPORT CARDS

VOTING   MOTHER'S DAY

GRADUATION

VALENTINE'S DAY

SNOW STORMS

TEAMING UP

You may find it difficult to come up with fresh ideas on a consistent basis. If so, team up with a friend who doesn't necessarily have skill in cartooning but does have a flair for stories and gags.

Working together, you can turn out a first-class product!

JOTTING DOWN THE IDEAS

You would be amazed at the number of terrific ideas that are lost or forgotten because people say to themselves, "I'll remember it when I get home (or to the office) and write it down then." But chances are that you won't be able to remember it. There is nothing worse than trying to figure out what the great gag was. It can drive you crazy!

NOTE PAD

Good ideas and jokes are too precious to lose. You never know when and where that award-winning gag is going to pop into your head, so be prepared! Develop the habit of carrying a pocket-size note pad with you at all times. Don't leave home without it! Also, don't forget a pen or pencil.

TAPE RECORDER

Another way to remember a thought is to carry a pocket-size micro-tape recorder. This is considerably more expensive than paper or pencil, but it is easier and faster to describe something by speaking than it is by writing. However, until you can afford a tape recorder, a note pad will do just fine.

DESIGNING YOUR
COMIC STRIP CHARACTERS

Your first task is to develop a theme that is familiar to you. Remember, you can write best about those things you know. Being totally familiar with a character and the situations he or she faces will make your writings more believable and authentic. Besides, you won't run out of material. It makes sense, right?

HERE ARE SOME THEMES TO CONSIDER:

Husband & Wife   Teenagers
Family   Aliens
Animals   Whatever!

The best way to create the characters for your strip is to make many sketches. Refine the features and proportions as you do each drawing. And, before you know it . . . there's the final sketch!

GOOD ONE!

Once you have decided on the subject matter, you can begin designing the characters. First, consider these points:

1. LIKABILITY—Your character must be pleasing to the eye. This applies especially to your main character. He or she must also be easily recognized. Think of your favorite comic strip character. You would know him or her anywhere!

2. SIMPLICITY—Your character must be relatively easy to draw and look the same from all angles. Remember, if you are fortunate enough to have your strip published, you will have to draw that character many times—hopefully, for years!

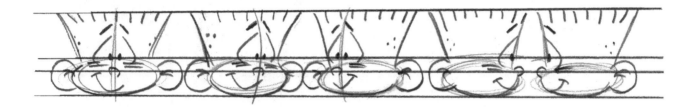

Notice how the features always fall on the same line in the sketch above. Also, note the relationship of the head size to the rest of the body in the illustration below.

191

ROUGHED OUT

This step takes your idea from your note pad or tape recorder and refines it into a comic strip. A comic strip is set up like a short movie or play—establish the premise, set up the gag, and BAM! . . . deliver the punch line.

You may be able to do this in two, three, or four panels. It will depend on the joke and your style of writing and drawing. Use as many panels as it takes to tell the story. The rough sketch can be done on any kind of paper. Remember, the sketch's only purpose is to be a point of reference while doing the finished drawing.

Since a comic strip is much like a movie or a play, you are much like a director. You are also the person who works the camera, chooses the cast, writes the screenplay . . . you do everything!

LET'S TAKE THIS STEP BY STEP:

1. Screenplay—You need to write the actual dialogue for the actors (characters) to say. Try to keep the words to a bare minimum—just enough to make the point.

2. Casting—You must decide which one of your cartoon characters is best-suited to star in the story and which ones are to be in the supporting cast.

3. Director—As the director you decide the best way to fill the frame (square or rectangular panel). This means selecting the proper angle from which to view the characters, and choosing the props and the location.

4. Camera—Just as the cameraman photographs what the director has decided upon, you, as the artist, have to draw it in.

PAPER SIZE

When I was a boy, I used to think that cartoonists drew the comic strip the same size as it appeared in the newspaper. I used to wonder how they got so much detail in such a small space! Now, I know that most cartoonists work on panels that are more than twice the reproduced size. This means that your lines must be able to withstand the reduction and not fade or break up.

ORIGINAL SIZE

NEWSPAPER SIZE

The size of the strip will vary from one cartoonist to another. Also, each newspaper prints the strips in different sizes. Check out the comic sections in different papers and see for yourself. A typical newspaper comic strip will measure approximately 6" x 1¾".

Here is a method for enlarging your comic strip while keeping the same ratio:

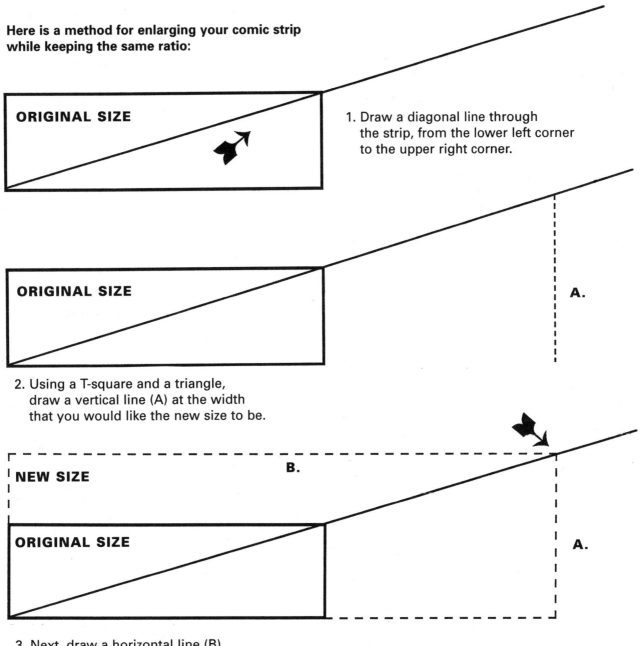

ORIGINAL SIZE

1. Draw a diagonal line through the strip, from the lower left corner to the upper right corner.

ORIGINAL SIZE

A.

2. Using a T-square and a triangle, draw a vertical line (A) at the width that you would like the new size to be.

NEW SIZE

B.

ORIGINAL SIZE

A.

3. Next, draw a horizontal line (B) to the vertical line (A), making sure they intersect on the diagonal line.

You can do this at any point on the diagonal line and it will be in correct proportion!

LETTERING

The lettering in your comic strip is just as important as the cartooning itself. Remember, it is the words that convey the message. Notice how many different styles of cartoon lettering there are in the comic section of your newspaper. Like cartooning, lettering requires many hours of practice for your own style to emerge. Most comic strip lettering is done in CAPITALS only. The lettering is first penciled in and then inked over. To ensure that there is enough room for all the words, the lettering is done first, and then the bubble, and then the cartoon. Remember, the letters must be legible, even after they are reduced—one good reason for keeping the message as short as possible.

ABCDEFGHIJKLMNOPQRSTUVWXYZ

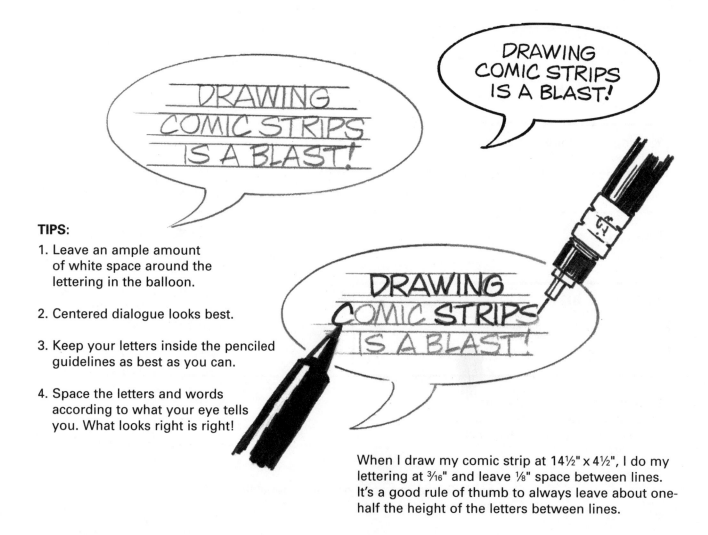

TIPS:

1. Leave an ample amount of white space around the lettering in the balloon.

2. Centered dialogue looks best.

3. Keep your letters inside the penciled guidelines as best as you can.

4. Space the letters and words according to what your eye tells you. What looks right is right!

When I draw my comic strip at 14½" x 4½", I do my lettering at ³⁄₁₆" and leave ⅛" space between lines. It's a good rule of thumb to always leave about one-half the height of the letters between lines.

BALLOON & LETTERING TRICKS

DON'T TELL ANYONE, BUT...

SPEAKING SOFTLY

THAT'S THE LAST STRAW!!

YELLING AT SOMEONE

TODAY'S WEATHER...

WORDS FROM TV, ANSWERING MACHINE, OR ANYTHING ELECTRIC.

DO **NOT** GO IN THERE!

BOLD WORD FOR EMPHASIS

I'M SORRY SNIFF

DIALOGUE WITH SOUND EFFECT

IT'S C-C-COLD IN HERE!

PERSON IS COLD

PICTURE THOUGHT BALLOON

SOUND EFFECTS:

WHEW

R-R-RING

BOING

GASP

MORE BALLOON TALK

It's natural for the reader's eye to begin reading from left to right. So, it's important to your gag or story to have the sequence of dialog also going from left to right, as shown here. Also notice that the balloon of the person speaking second is positioned a little lower, too.

There are many styles of balloons in comic strips. This one to the right shows the balloon extending past the frame or panel.

This balloon also extends beyond the frame or panel, and is drawn to look fluffy like a cloud.

This balloon is drawn within the frame and has a tone behind it to make it stand out.

This balloon also is within the frame, but has a pattern drawn behind it.

The balloons and lettering you choose, like everything else in cartooning, all depend on your style.

PANEL LAYOUTS

Here are some suggestions of how to lay out your panel or frame in order to tell your story with maximum effect.

CLOSE UP

EXTREME CLOSE UP

MEDIUM

CHARACTER IN SILHOUETTE

MEDIUM LONGSHOT

This is used when it's important to show a lot of the background and character; to establish the background and setting.

PANEL DO'S AND DON'TS

1. In this panel we have two characters speaking, drawn from below the waist. The main action is in the facial expressions and hand movements. The rest is wasted.

2. By zooming in and focusing on their faces, shoulders, and one hand, it is much more effective.

1. This panel shows the opposite of above. We are too close, and are missing the effect of the fellow jumping.

2. By pulling back and revealing his entire body, we let his body language and the other character's reaction tell the story much better.

STEP BY STEP COMIC STRIP

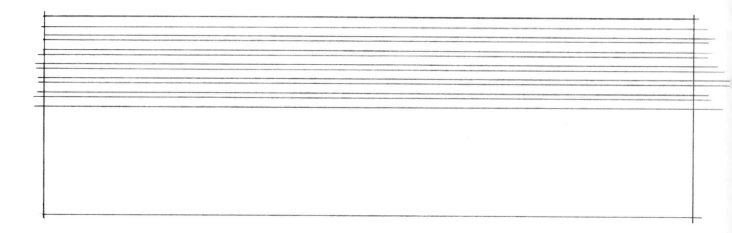

STEP 1

• Use an HB or #2 pencil.

• Measure out your strip (14½" wide and 4¼" high).

• Rule out your guidelines for the lettering. Use a T-square and a triangle to make sure they are parallel. Make the guidelines ³⁄₁₆" apart for the words and ⅛" apart (or half the size of the letters) for the space between the lines.

¼" MARGIN BETWEEN PANELS

STEP 2

• Using your "rough layout" as a reference, pencil in the words and the cartooning. Then divide the strip into panels. I use an HB pencil or a #2 pencil for this. If you use a pencil that is too hard, it will dig into the paper; a pencil that is too soft will get too messy to work with.

TIP: If you have trouble with the composition of a panel and cannot get it to look quite right, simply approach the problem from a different direction. There are many ways to "fill up" the panel to get the story told.

STEP 3

• Ink in the lettering, the balloons, and the borders. If you are satisfied with the cartooning, go ahead and ink it in as well. (Use pen and ink or markers for this step.)

STEP 4

• Make sure the ink is completely dry, then use your kneaded rubber eraser to erase the pencil lines.

• Check over the comic strip for any lines you may have forgotten to draw and add them. Also, make sure that the lines you have drawn will withstand the reduction and not fade out.

STEP 5

• Fill in any large black areas there might be in your comic strip. Use a brush and ink or a black marker with a large nib. Black areas help tie the composition together, so figure out the best way to use them in your own style.

WHITE TAPE

OPAQUE WHITE PAINT

STEP 6

• Go back over the strip and correct any mistakes.
You can use opaque white paint and a small brush for this;
however, sometimes markers and felt-tip pens will bleed
through, so be careful. If this happens, you can use
white masking tape. Cut small pieces of this tape with
an art knife and place it over the mistakes and smudges.

HERE'S A TRICK TO COMPARE YOUR STRIP WITH THE PROS!

The comic strips you see in the newspaper are reduced by a machine called a "photostat camera," which is a very expensive piece of equipment. However, there is good news! With the new, advanced photocopy machines, you can go to a local "quick printer" and reduce your artwork for a fraction of the cost. The quality will depend on the individual copier; but generally, it will look pretty good.

1. Reduce your original comic strip artwork to newspaper size. (You may have to do this in two steps.)

2. Trim the reduced strip right up to the borders and use rubber cement to stick it over another comic strip in the newspaper.

3. Next, use 11" x 17" paper and photocopy the whole comic section (or as much as you can fit in the copy area) at 100%.

Now your comic strip blends in with the rest of the strips and you can compare your style with the pros! It's always a kick to see your cartooning when it is smaller because the reduction "tightens up" your drawing and makes it look more professional. Also, this is a good way to see if your lines are able to withstand the reduction.

• PRACTICE BY STUDYING OTHER CARTOONISTS WHOSE STYLES YOU ADMIRE (EVERYBODY LEARNS THIS WAY). YOUR OWN STYLE WILL EVENTUALLY DEVELOP ALL BY ITSELF!

• KEEP THE SUBJECT MATTER OF YOUR COMIC STRIP CLEAN AND GENERAL, ESPECIALLY IF YOU WANT TO APPEAL TO A BROAD AUDIENCE. DON'T WRITE AND DRAW ABOUT DRUGS OR OTHER BAD HABITS UNLESS IT IS TO PRESENT THEM IN A NEGATIVE WAY (FOR EXAMPLE: A CARTOON DONE FOR A PUBLIC SERVICE POSTER OR A COMMUNITY NEWSLETTER).

• KEEP A SKETCH PAD AND PENCIL WITH YOU WHEREVER YOU GO.

WELCOME TO THE FABULOUS WORLD OF COMIC BOOK HEROES! HERE, YOU CAN MAKE UP STORIES THAT YOU BRING TO LIFE WITH YOUR OWN HEROES, SUPPORTING CAST, AND PROPS. IT'S GREAT FUN TO KNOW THAT OTHERS ENJOY YOUR WORK, AND THAT YOUR DRAWINGS AND WORDS CAN STIR UP MANY EMOTIONS. ALL OF THIS WILL REQUIRE A LOT OF WORK AND A LOT OF TIME, BUT IT WILL BE VERY REWARDING . . . IF YOU STICK WITH IT!

SO, IF YOU'RE READY TO MAKE THIS WORLD A SAFER PLACE, I'LL TURN YOU OVER TO MY PAL, BRUCE, TO SHOW YOU HOW.

HERO GUY

WRITING A STORY

Without a story, there is no reason to pick up a pencil and draw. If writing stories is something that doesn't come easily to you as drawing, perhaps you can collaborate with a friend, as I said in the Comic Strip chapter.

Your reader should be served a story just like he's at a banquet—with four tantalizing courses. The courses your story should have:

1. **START**—This is where you establish the setting—the location and the mood—as well as the cast of characters that will be acting in the story.
2. **MIDDLE**—Here is where you build to a conflict. For example, the bad guy doing his thing to cause some sort of havoc.
3. **PEAK**—This is where the villain gets it! The good guy triumphs over evil.
4. **RESOLUTION**—After your (hopefully exciting) tale of heroics, everything returns to normal.

ROUGHING OUT

This is where you turn your story into a script, with actual dialogue. It's a good idea to keep your dialogue as short as possible, but without losing the meaning of what you want to say. Also, this is where you decide how many panels it will take to tell your story, and how to best lay it out.

MOTIVATIONAL TIP

Don't be afraid to start drawing. The worst mistake you could make would be not to try.

GULP!

HERO HEADS

All cartoons are not created equal! Drawing hero heads is a little different than the "bubble-nose" variety of cartooning. Below we have an example of each type.

COMIC STYLE—In comic style cartooning, there are no rules. There are many styles for stretching the features, as shown throughout this book. It's more humorous than realistic.

HERO STYLE—Hero-style cartooning requires a more realistic approach. It is based upon drawing human features and proportions the way they actually are, but stylizing them a bit.

STEP-BY-STEP MALE HERO HEAD

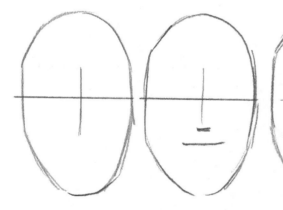

STEP 1. Draw an egg-shape with the narrow end at the bottom. Draw two guidelines that meet in the center of the shape.

STEP 2. Draw a line a little more than halfway from the bottom to the center, and another line a bit longer just below. You now have the basis to draw a hero head. The rest is easy.

STEP 3. Place the eyes on the horizontal guideline. Draw eyebrows just above to give expression. Draw a line for the nose to one side of the vertical guideline. Make the line under the mouth thick to give the illusion of depth to the lower lip.

STEP 4. Add some details to the features, like lines around the nose for nostrils. Draw in the ears to be approximately equal with the bottom of the nose. Define the jawbone just under the ears to give him a strong look.

STEP 5. Draw in some detail, like two curved lines for defined cheekbones, and a light line or two under the lower lip to bring out the chin . . . and of course, hair! Draw his hair past the outline of his head because it has thickness and mass.

FEMALE HERO HEAD

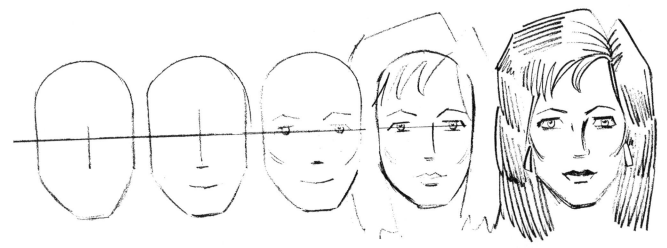

UP

RIGHT

FACING IN DIFFERENT DIRECTIONS

As before with comic heads, we get them to look in different directions by thinking of the object as a three-dimensional shape, and by wrapping the guidelines around as shown here.

DOWN

LEFT

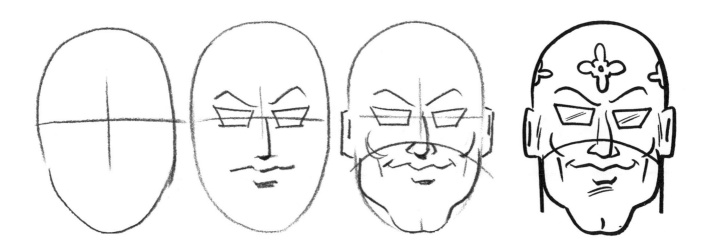

219

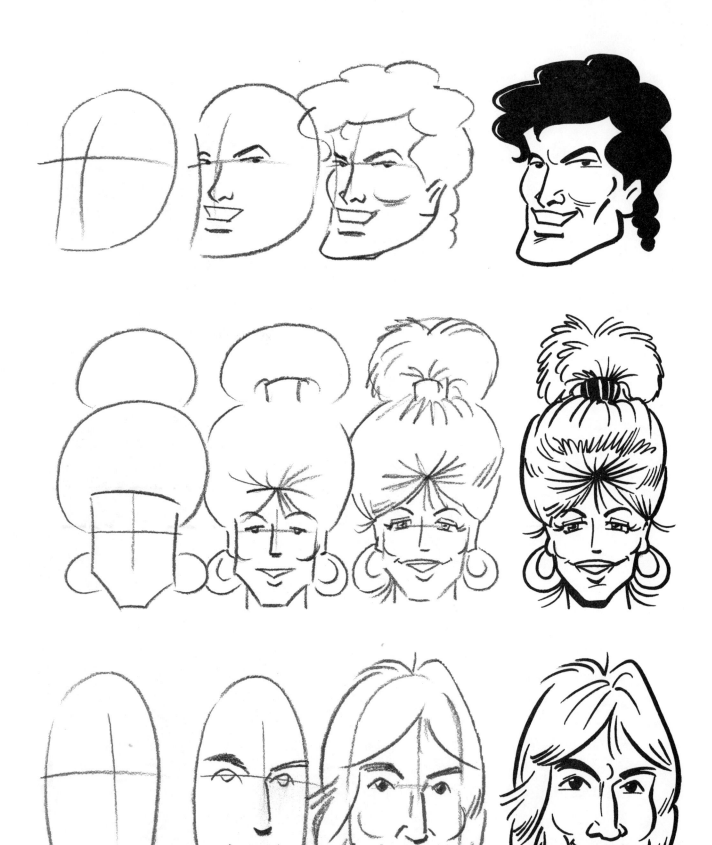

221

SUPPORTING CAST

These are the people that help tell your story. What I like to do is to sketch some faces. By looking at them, I get story ideas of who they may be and what they might do. It's great fun to let your imagination run loose. Here are some examples:

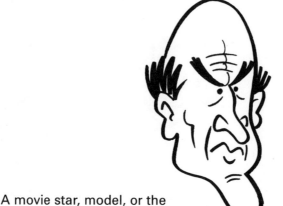

Here we have a face that could easily be cast as a miser, heartless banker, or evil landlord.

A movie star, model, or the love interest of the male hero.

This face works well as someone's grandmother or the neighborhood gossip.

This fellow could be cast as the delivery man, postal worker, baseball coach, or a friendly neighbor down the street.

No story is complete without the ever-present police commissioner who is a little bit grumpy, but has a very kind heart.

This woman could be the computer expert who breaks a code; a doctor, lawyer, teacher, or secretary who didn't trust the stranger from the very first time he set foot in the office.

This little boy could be cast as an eyewitness to the crime who calls the police, or the boy who needs to be rescued.

EXPRESSION

The characters' facial expression helps to convey
what is happening in the story, even without words!

BAD TASTING **GAZING** **LAUGHING** **ANGRY**

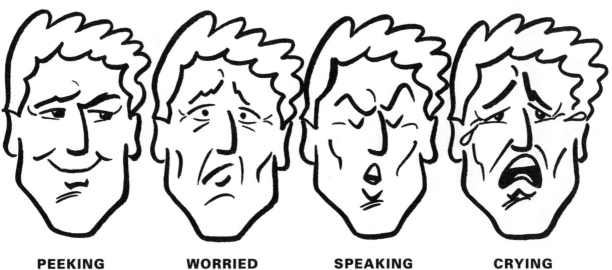

PEEKING **WORRIED** **SPEAKING** **CRYING**

I'VE GOT TO FIND HER GRANDSON!

HERO GUY

SNIFF

A great practice exercise is to create situations with two or more characters reacting to each other, using the appropriate expressions and dialog.

HERO BODIES

Meet Hero Guy! As you can see, he is 8 heads tall. The proportion in which you draw your character is totally up to you; however, be familiar with these proportions so that you can draw him the same each time.

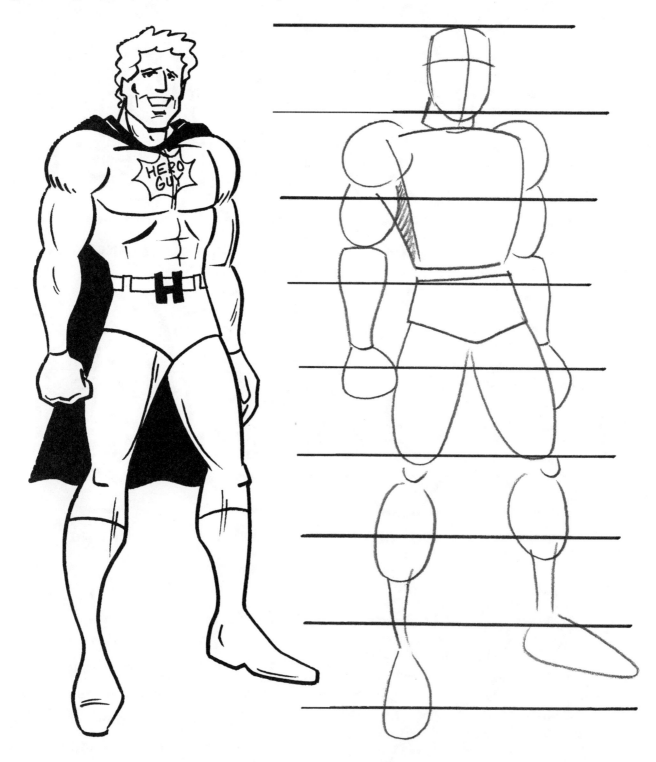

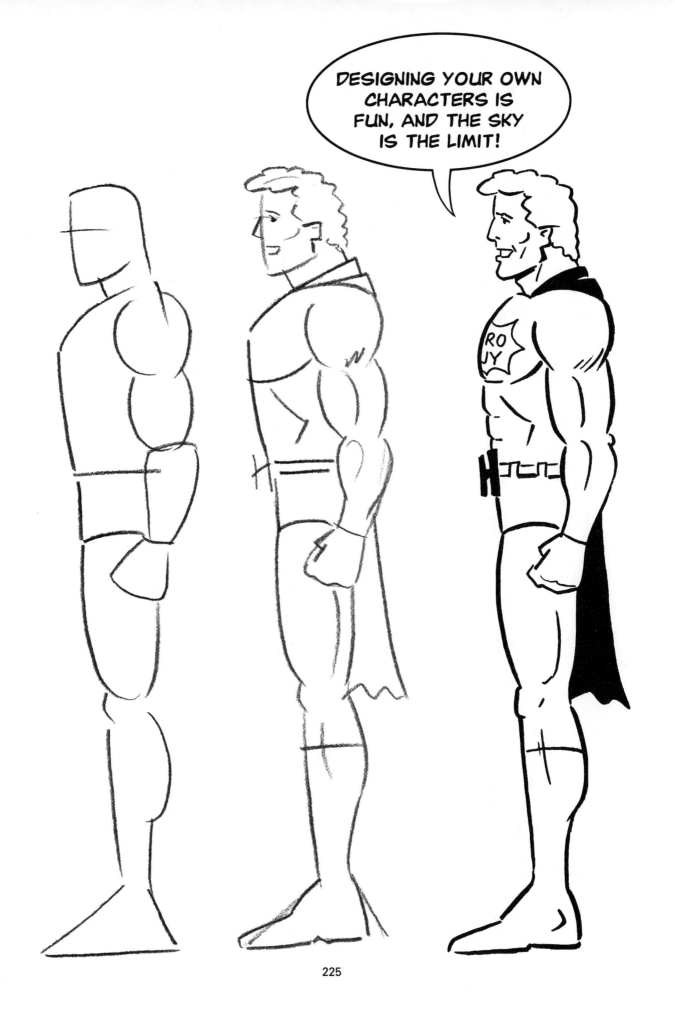

Meet Hero Gal! She, too, is about 8 heads tall (not including her hair!). Notice that in both male and female characters, the elbow is around waist level and the hands fall around the middle of the thigh.

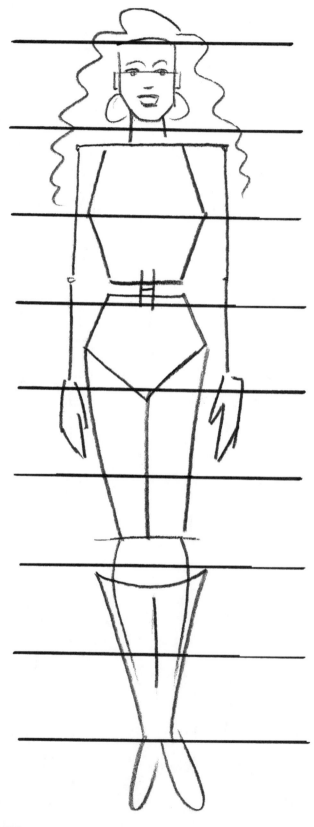

As you can see, I have constructed these bodies
by combining the stick-figure with shapes.

LIFTING

TAKE-OFF

FOR PRACTICE,
"ROUGH OUT"
FIGURES IN
VARIOUS ACTIONS
LIKE THESE.

PUNCHING

READY FOR
ACTION

228

FLYING

PRACTICE IS THE KEY TO SUCCESS!

THROWING

LEAPING

RUNNING (HERO-SPEED)

FLYING

Remember to use "cartoon effects"
to illustrate the character
"swooshing" through the air.

By drawing his head a littler smaller than usual, his body appears larger and more massive.

**GOOD GUY OR BAD GUY? . . .
YOU DECIDE.**

231

The slanted black line here shows
the basic line of motion, which,
in this case, shows the character
leaning forward as she runs.

Notice that her arms and legs
are in opposite motion.

232

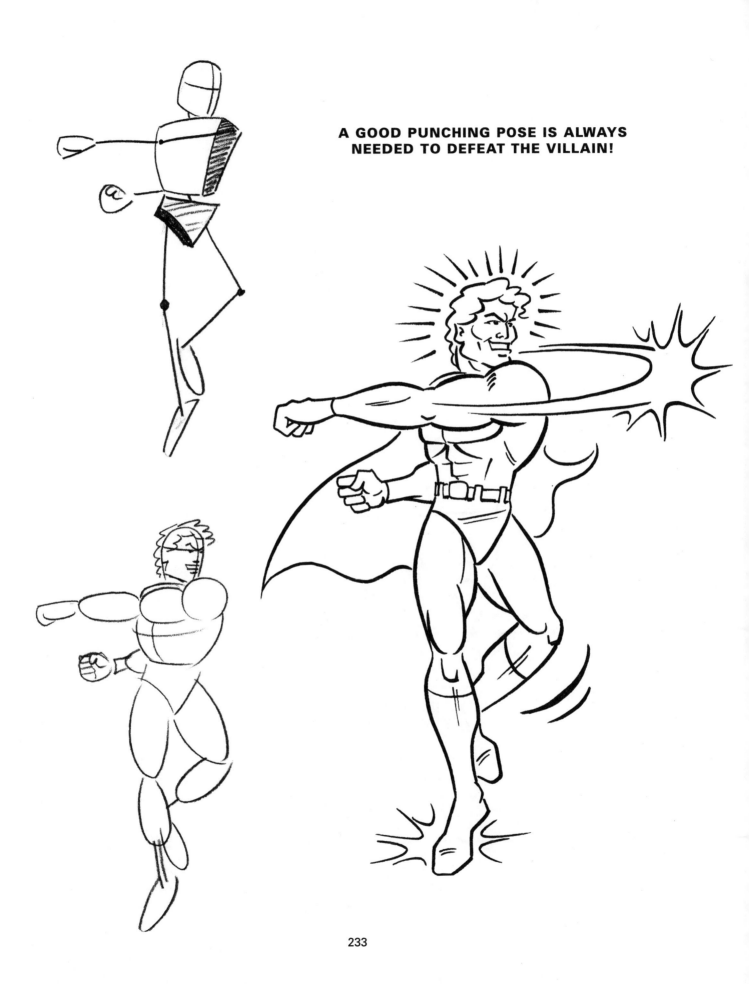

A GOOD PUNCHING POSE IS ALWAYS NEEDED TO DEFEAT THE VILLAIN!

LIFTING

STYLIZED HEROES

Create stylized heroes by using less lines and detail in drawing, like with the two guys on this page. They also are more "cartoonified," which means that their proportions are unrealistic.

HUMAN BEAN SHAPE

POWER PERSON

WHO ARE YOU CALLIN' UNREALISTIC?

HYPER HERO

235

CAMERA ANGLES

A comic book is very much like a movie, and you must design the panel or frame so that the viewer understands the sequence of events in the story—this keeps them interested enough to want to continue reading. Here are some panel designs:

Long vertical panel with someone speaking from inside the building.

Extreme Close-up. This fella, by appearing large in the foreground, conveys an extra measure of tension.

Looking Up. Here we have the person in distress looking up at what looks to be "Toaster-Head Man." This makes the villain appear scarier.

Medium Close-up. The characters are the main focus of the frame. Little or no background is needed.

Looking Down. Here we use what we have learned about perspective to achieve the effect of looking down from the roof-top, or perhaps while flying.

MOTIVATIONAL TIP

Have Goals! If you aim
at nothing . . .
you are sure to hit it!

SIZE

Earlier, we learned how to reduce your cartoons to comic strip size—now we'll tackle comic *book* size. It's much easier to draw a comic book page by working larger than the finished printed size (which is usually about 6½" x 10¼"). Here is a method for reducing your cartoon to comic-book size while keeping the same ratio:

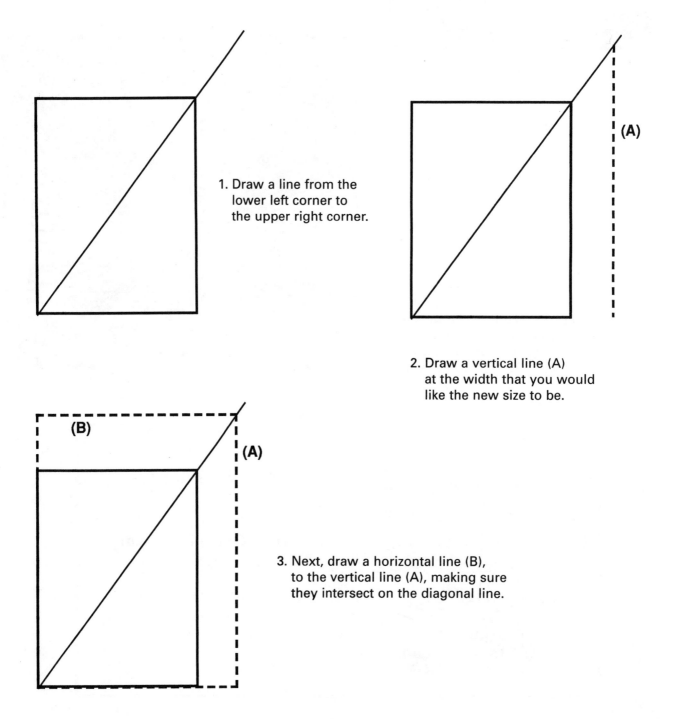

1. Draw a line from the lower left corner to the upper right corner.

2. Draw a vertical line (A) at the width that you would like the new size to be.

3. Next, draw a horizontal line (B), to the vertical line (A), making sure they intersect on the diagonal line.

Here is the cartoon panel at its original size.

Here is the same panel reduced to comic book size. Notice how the cartoon lines withstand reduction without fading or breaking up.

PENCILING

Pencil in the borders, lettering guidelines, characters, and backgrounds. Refer to your rough layout for the dialogue and panel composition you've decided upon to tell the story.

ACTUAL SIZE

INKING

Go over your pencil lines and make one definite outline. Be sure that your lines are thick enough to withstand the reduction to actual comic book size. Also, try to vary your hand pressure when using your pen or marker—try to get a thick and thin quality to your line. This will make your cartoon more professional and more interesting to look at!

REDUCED TO COMIC BOOK SIZE

CLEANED UP

Make sure that all the ink lines are dry so that you can erase over the entire drawing without smearing your work. The pencil lines disappear and the ink lines stay. Now you can fix any mistakes that remain.

Use white opaque paint to cover mistakes.

Use white tape here to cover this line that extended past the border.

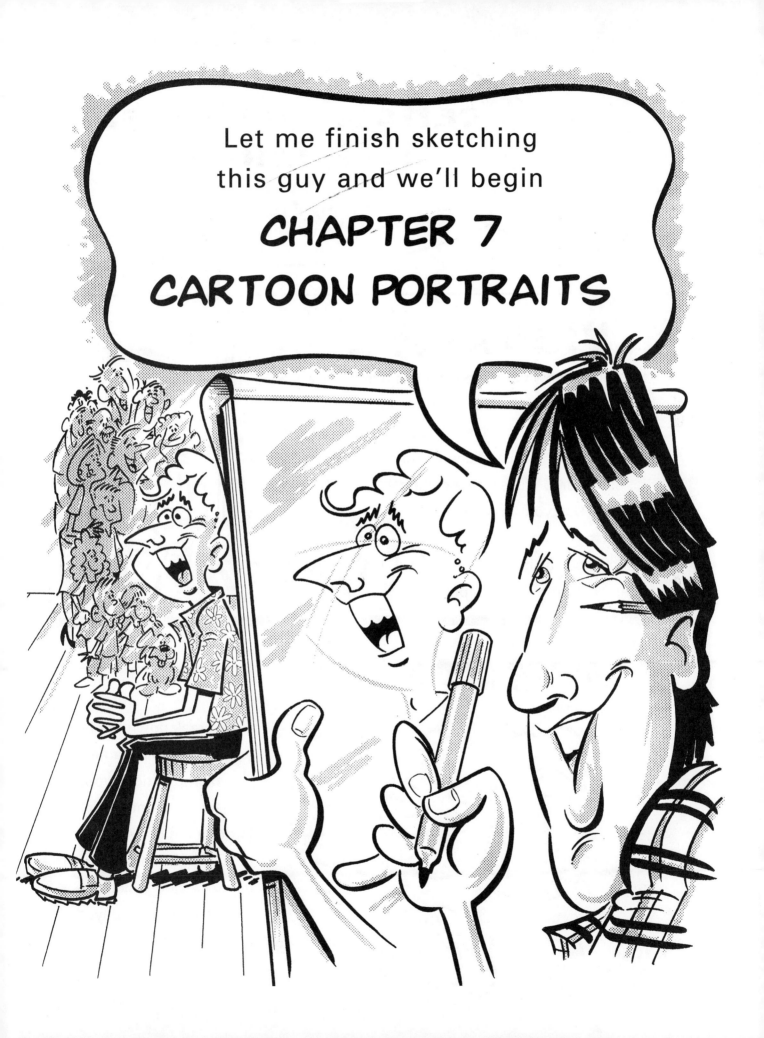

To draw cartoon portraits... look into my **IZE** !

1. VISUAL**IZE**

Think about how your subject looks over-all. We all know that no two people look exactly alike (except twins!), but after drawing many people you will find that each person falls into a certain category. Use your imagination, and try to picture your subject's face as if it were already drawn on your paper.

2. SUMMAR**IZE**

FACIAL SHAPE   FEATURES

H-M-M-M

Now break down the features into basic elements. For example, does your subject have unusually large or small eyes? Thin or full lips? A big or small nose? Decide which features should be "played up" or "played down."

3. REAL**IZE**

Now, using pencil, try to create a realistic likeness of the subject. Certain aspects of his or her face will automatically stand out, inviting you to exaggerate them.

4. STYL**IZE**

Working with a marker or pen forces you to draw a single, definite, black line. This helps make the features look "cartoonified," so the drawing automatically becomes "stylized."

5. HUMOR**IZE**

Cartoon portraits are supposed to be fun, so add a humorous setting, props, and clothing to indicate the subject's occupation or favorite sport, hobby, or fantasy. These details help to "personalize" the drawing.

HELENE

SKETCHING FROM PHOTOGRAPHS

FRONTAL VIEW

The frontal view is the most difficult view to draw because the facial features have to match up. Nobody's face is perfectly symmetrical, but it should be fairly close.

1. First, sketch the subject's overall facial shape—and be loose! If you are working with pencil at this stage, you don't have to worry about committing yourself to anything because you can always erase!

2. Next, draw in some guidelines for the placement of the features. When drawing the features, look for shapes within the face (in this case, on the photograph). For example, notice the small ovals on the cheeks and the diamond shape that forms around the mouth.

3. When you are happy with the sketch, go over it with a marker. Don't try to follow the pencil lines exactly; just use them as guides. If you try to follow the pencil lines too closely, the drawing will look "stiff." Don't forget to add a background or some props to enhance the character.

This is a more exaggerated version of the same face.

SIDE VIEW

The side-view, or "profile," is probably the easiest view to draw because you don't have to worry about making the features equal. For example, you don't have to be concerned with matching the eye widths, the ear sizes, the sides of the face, and so on. You have fewer features to work with, however, so you must make them count or you won't achieve a likeness.

1. You have to begin some where, so I begin with the bridge of the nose and work down to the tip.

2. Draw in the upper lip.

3. Then draw in the front line of the teeth and the bottom lip.

4. Now draw the chin and part of the neck, and then stop.

5. The line that outlines the cheek is impor- tant because it tells you where to place the eye.

6. Notice that the eye rests on top of the cheek. Also, draw the eye brow; it is critical to the subject's expression.

7. Draw the top of the head. You can be a bit more "sketchy" here because you can incorporate the lines into the hair.

8. Be sure to make the head big enough. People who are just starting out often fail to draw this curved line back far enough.

1. First draw in the guidelines. These lines establish the angle of the subject's head.

2. Loosely "rough out" the features, and then refine.

THREE-QUARTER VIEW

This view can be more difficult than the profile, but the angle of the eyes adds more personality. It can be easier than the frontal view because you don't have to match up the features.

3. Notice that the hair is filled in to create the shape of the side of the face. This technique allows you to adjust the outline of the face until you are satisfied with it; you can fill in or erase as needed.

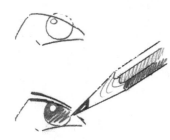

Notice how part of the eye is hidden under the upper eyelid. Sometimes, depending on the tilt of the face, the eye circle is hidden by the lower lid, and sometimes it's hidden by a bit of both lids. This subject has dark eyes, so I filled in the eye except for the small white highlight.

There's no rule that says you have to use a marker for your final drawing. This one was done with an HB drawing pencil.

248

At first glance, I saw the shape above with the facial features placed in a relatively small area within the dotted lines (left).

The drawing above was done with a large bullet-point marker; it is shown reduced to 50% of its original size.

BARLEY

249

This drawing is based on
a square. Notice the defined
circles that make up the cheeks.

This sketch was done with
an ordinary #2 pencil.

This sketch is a bit less
cartoonified than
the previous examples.

PRACTICE TIP #9

Practice sketching directly from the
television. The camera moves on and
off the actor's face so rapidly that you
are forced to develop the technique
of quickly picking out the critical points
of likeness. Don't worry if you don't
complete these drawings; they're
simply drills for sharpening your skills.

SKETCHING FROM LIVE SUBJECTS

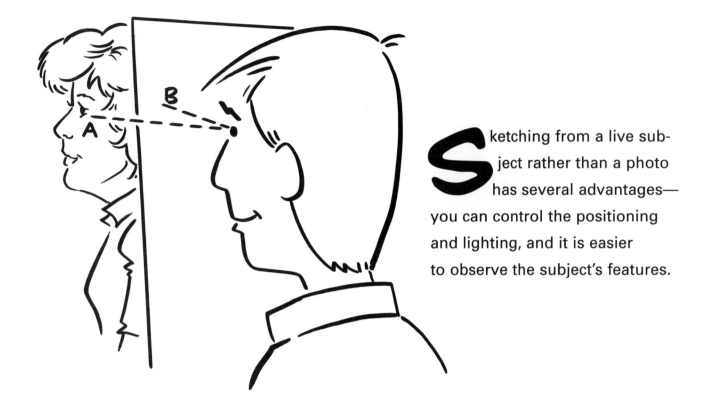

Sketching from a live subject rather than a photo has several advantages—you can control the positioning and lighting, and it is easier to observe the subject's features.

HERE'S AN INTERESTING TECHNIQUE

Position the subject so his or her face is just showing from the left side of the edge of your drawing pad, as shown in the illustration above. (Note: if you are left handed, position the subject to the right of your drawing pad and facing the opposite direction.) The distance between the subject's face and the drawing surface should be just a slight movement of your eye.

Now for the trick: glance at one of the features on your model's face and take a mental "picture" of it. The picture can then be "developed" when you move your eye back to the paper, which is only about an inch away. Visualize the feature on the paper and draw it immediately. This trick works great but only for a few seconds at a time; then it fades. It works because the subject and the drawing surface are so close to each other.

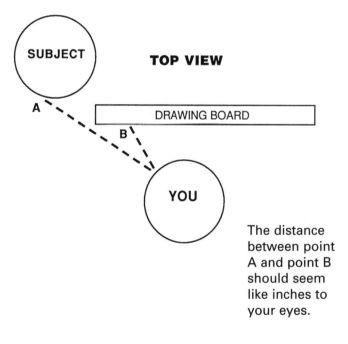

The distance between point A and point B should seem like inches to your eyes.

MORE SKETCHES FROM PHOTOGRAPHS

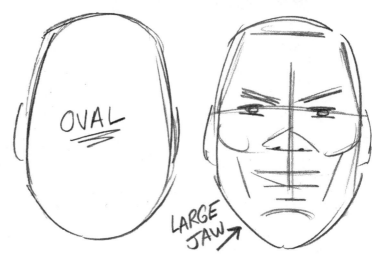

OVAL

LARGE JAW →

This subject has a classic, oval-shaped head. Start with the basic shape, and then add guidelines for the features. Try to capture a likeness by exaggerating the most prominent features. Notice that I didn't draw each tooth—I merely indicated the overall shape.

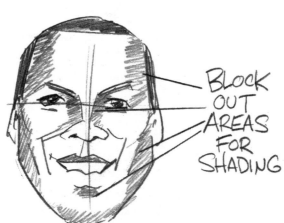

BLOCK OUT AREAS FOR SHADING

This sketch was done by softening the pencil strokes with a paper stump, as illustrated here.

Another way to use a paper stump is to first rub some pencil on a separate piece of paper, stroke the tip of the paper stump into the graphite, and then use the stump as a drawing tool. This technique produces a softer, blended tone.

This subject begins with a squarish shape.

Leave white gaps in the hair
to indicate highlights.

The upper lip is not pronounced,
so I just drew it as a heavy black line.

The final drawing was done with a large tip marker.

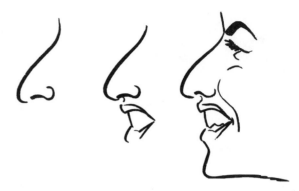

Sweep in the lines with one definite stroke! Go for it! Even if it doesn't come out quite right, it will have authority—this is sometimes better than drawing it correctly but weakly.

Sometimes I draw the overall outline of the hair and then fill it in. (Notice how large I have drawn the head!)

GONE WITH THE BREEZE

This subject likes to read!

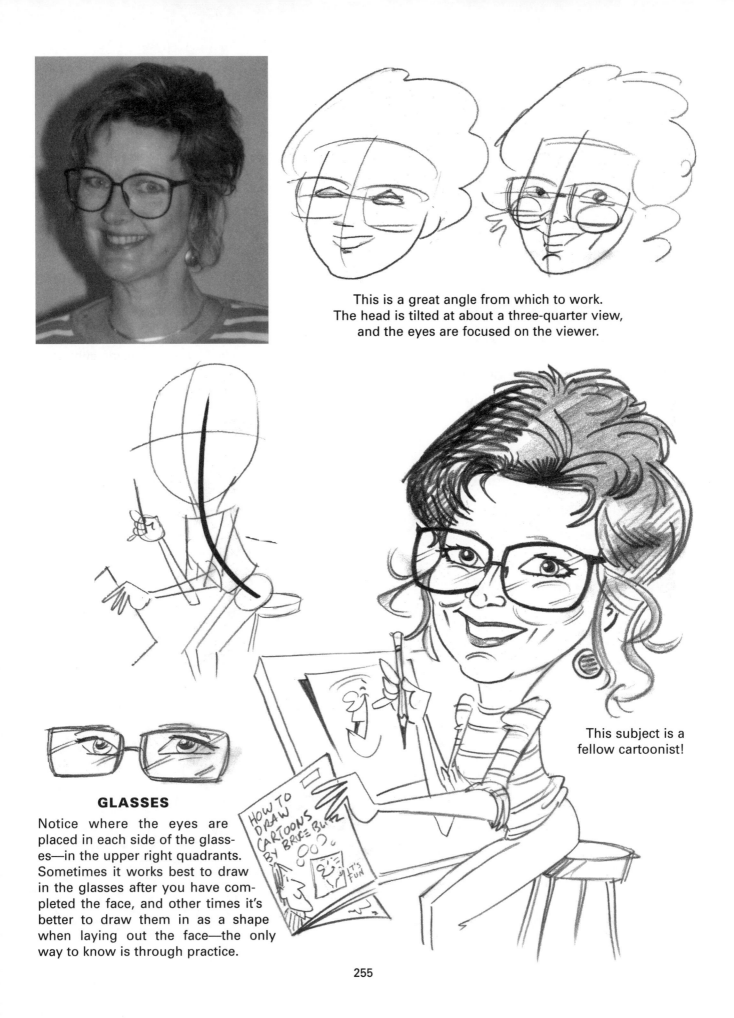

This is a great angle from which to work.
The head is tilted at about a three-quarter view,
and the eyes are focused on the viewer.

This subject is a
fellow cartoonist!

GLASSES

Notice where the eyes are placed in each side of the glasses—in the upper right quadrants. Sometimes it works best to draw in the glasses after you have completed the face, and other times it's better to draw them in as a shape when laying out the face—the only way to know is through practice.

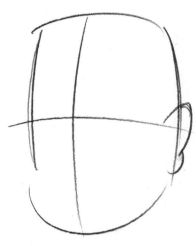

The eyebrows are a critical point of likeness for this distinguished-looking subject.

First, try to see the beard as a shape; then, lightly sketch the outline. Make any necessary changes and fill it in. It's not necessary to draw each strand of hair in a beard or mustache—simply suggest the direction the hair is taking, as shown in the final drawing.

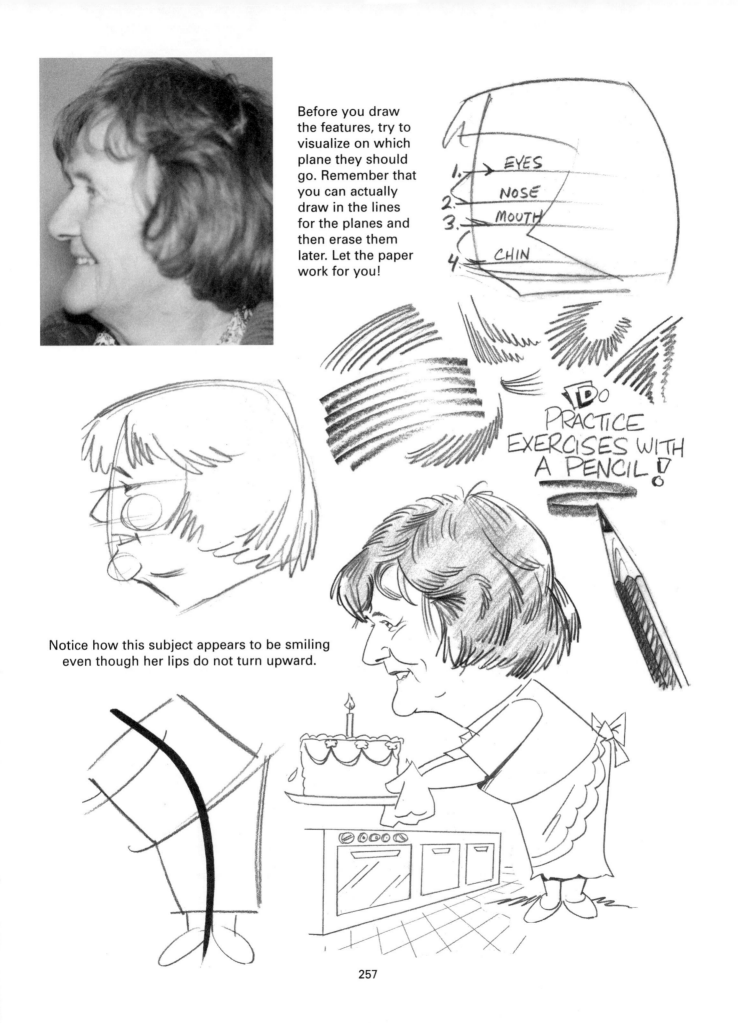

Before you draw the features, try to visualize on which plane they should go. Remember that you can actually draw in the lines for the planes and then erase them later. Let the paper work for you!

1. EYES
2. NOSE
3. MOUTH
4. CHIN

DO PRACTICE EXERCISES WITH A PENCIL!

Notice how this subject appears to be smiling even though her lips do not turn upward.

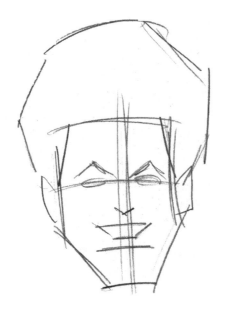

Remember: First go for
a likeness, then simplify—
"cartoon-style."

When doodling, look for a basic theme to follow.
In this case, I went with sharp angles for the face—and,
of course, the high hair made this a fun subject to caricature.

DIRECTION OF
THE PENCIL STROKES
DETERMINES THE
DIRECTION THE HAIR
IS COMBED.

GET YOUR OWN
CONCEPT OF THE PHOTOS
IN THIS BOOK... BE
ORIGINAL! USE THE
ILLUSTRATIONS AS A
LEARNING GUIDE.

When drawing
little guys like
this fellow artist,
you must be careful
not to place the chin
too far from the lower lip.
If you do, the subject
will appear much older.

PRACTICE TIP #10

Sketch from photos in magazines.
They offer fine practice because
they are generally a good size, clear,
and usually in color (although
black-and-white photos work just as well).

To draw a stylized caricature like me... just use less lines and see...

It is always best to draw your subjects when they're smiling! When someone smiles, their facial muscles make the cheek bones "round out," give prominence to the teeth, and bring life to the eyes. These factors all make drawing—and the result—much more interesting.

Here, the sweep of the mouth line is a good example of how to "play-up" a feature that's not on both sides of the face.

Details, such as the cleft in the strong chin, give your cartoon portraits an extra bit of character.

PRACTICE TIP #II

Ask your friends and family members to pose for you. This way, you can position them to practice drawing frontal, profile, and three-quarter views.

Sometimes I approach the drawing from a different perspective. In this case, I decided to start with the hair and work down because I feel the hair is the subject's most prominent feature.

TIP

STOP

LOOK

THINK

DRAW!

A heavy black marker worked especially well for this subject.

In the photo, you can actually see the subject's eyes; but I chose instead to draw the eyes as heavy lines—this adds to the overall smiling expression.

262

The entire shape of the head must be taken into consideration when laying out the drawing, which, in this case, includes the hairstyle.

When you are working with a black marker or felt-tip pen, it's easy to inadvertently draw the lines too heavy at times. Be careful not to bear down too hard on the pen. It's important to keep the features delicate, especially when drawing a pretty, young girl like this.

Teeth—It's not necessary to draw each tooth separately. By this I mean that you don't have to draw the lines that separate them. They usually don't look quite right if you do. Notice how I've drawn the outline of the bottom of the teeth and the outline of the gum line; the viewer's eye then fills in the connection. There may be times, however, when you are doing a more exaggerated type of caricature and you will want to accentuate the teeth. It all depends on the cartoon assignment and, of course, your individual style of cartooning.

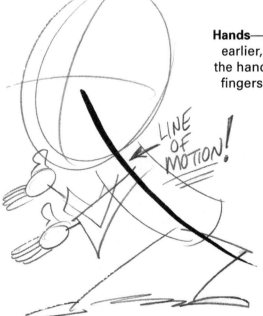

LINE OF MOTION!

Hands—As discussed earlier, notice how the hands are simply fingers on a circle!

Bob Noble

Eyelashes—When drawing blonde eyelashes, I have found that it works best not to have the hairs actually touch the eyelids. Notice how much lighter the hairs appear.

Filling in both sides of this subject's smile helped to give the drawing a greater feeling of depth. Also, notice the subtle differences between each side of the face.

SCRIPT

PRACTICE TIP #12

Family photos are great for sharpening your skills. However, look for pictures in which the person's head isn't tilted at an awkward angle because this makes it difficult to achieve a good likeness.

FAMILY PHOTOS

T he stick-figure method for drawing cartoon bodies has been around for many years, and I think it's a good way to lay down a basic structure. I like to add to the technique, however, by using shapes as well. Also, don't forget those extra little cartoon effects and accessories around the figure that create movement.

SQUARE

WHEELS ARE CYLINDERS

SCREEEECH

266

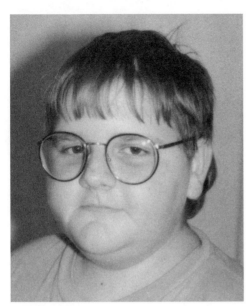

Notice the basic shapes
that were used to
draw this character.
It really is that easy!

Here is another example in which I decided to play down some features, such as the mouth and the nose, and play up other features, such as the glasses and the facial shape. This guy was a great subject!

Remember, cartoon portraits are supposed to be fun—they're not supposed to offend anyone. So make your pencil a friend to everyone!

CHOING
CHOING
CHOING

BOP

Funny sound effects add humor to the overall scene.

CARICATURES FOR EDITORIAL CARTOONS

Drawing caricatures of well-known political figures has been popular for many years and can be seen in political cartoons on the editorial page of your newspaper. Usually, the style used in these drawings is exaggerated much more than the kind used when drawing cartoon portraits for souvenirs. The extreme exaggeration helps to make the point of the cartoon more biting and satirical.

LET'S CARICATURE SOME PEOPLE FROM DAYS GONE BY

This is fun to do! There are many historical figures who are recognizable because of their hairstyle, clothing, outstanding facial features, or accessories. A crisp, stylized sketch of one of these characters can come in handy for school assignments—and they are especially good for advertising situations!

BENJAMIN FRANKLIN

Here is a good example of using a classic running pose to illustrate the point of your cartoon.

ABRAHAM LINCOLN

ONE

TWO

O nce you are familiar with the features of a particular face, you can draw the face in various positions and with different expressions, as shown below.

THREE

FOURSCORE AND SEVEN YEARS AGO . . .

LAUGHING

SICK

ANGRY

271

GEORGE WASHINGTON

He cannot tell a lie.

Can this be the way
it really happened?

This is an example of a typical quick-sketch caricature. The actual size can vary, but a good, all-around paper is either 9" x 12" or 11" x 14". The sketch is usually done in the profile view because it is easier and faster!

QUICK-SKETCH CARICATURES

These types of cartoon portraits are done quickly—usually in front of large groups of people. They are done directly with a marker, and depending on how much or how little detail is put into the drawing, they are usually completed in three to ten minutes each. These quick caricatures are a terrific source of fun and profit for cartoonists. It's as if people are actually commissioning you to do an original piece of artwork—but it takes you only a few minutes!

ELEMENTS OF A QUICK SKETCH

Quick sketch bodies are often done with "stock" bodies and gags—that is, standard poses for common sports, hobbies, and occupations. The baseball setting and gag below could be reworked in different ways by simply changing the expression of the guy on the left or by adding an expression of "knocked out" to the ball that was just hit. It's important to develop a wide variety of "stock" bodies and gags—especially if you plan to work in front of large crowds. This way, they won't see the same gag over and over again!

Subject's name in cartoon lettering.

You can use this space to add extra statistics about the subject, such as awards won, records held, or even a nickname.

An extra cartoon character helps to complete the gag.

The subject's head is the main focus of the drawing.

The body is usually done without much detail. (It can even be done with fewer lines than shown here.) The size will vary depending on your style, but the body is usually about one-half to one-third of the entire figure.

Draw just enough lines to establish the scene.

Customers usually like you to sign and date the drawing. This helps them to remember the good time they had on their vacation, at a friend's party, etc.

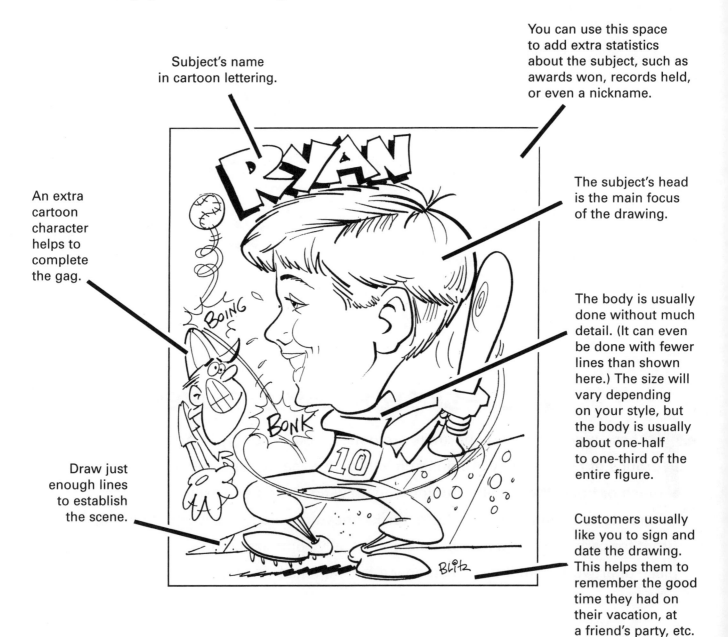

THREE STANDING POSES
FOR QUICK SKETCHES

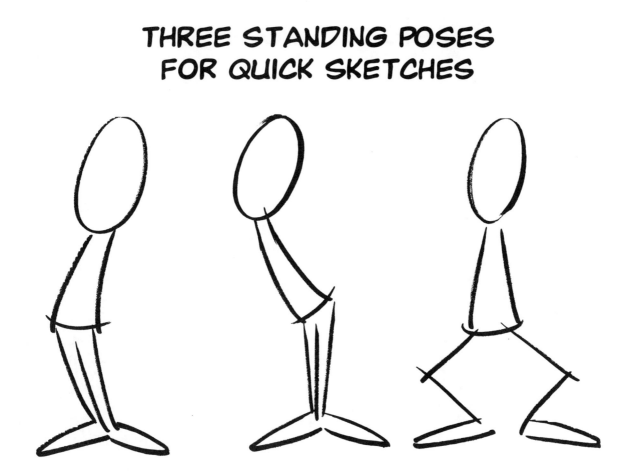

By simply changing the arms, clothing, and props,
this figure can work for many different situations.

LAWYER

GOLFER

WEIGHT
LIFTER

BASIC SITTING POSE

ARTIST

SEAMSTRESS

READER

BASIC RUNNING POSE

This is a versatile pose because it can be used for many different actions. Notice the little sign posts in these drawings; they can be used in a variety of ways to enhance the setting. Also, the "thought balloon" can add an extra touch of humor to the character.

Here are several more body poses that can be used for various actions.

VIDEO GAME PLAYER

FISHERMAN

PIANO PLAYER

BALLERINA

DIVER

WATER SKIER

BOWLER

CHEERLEADER

DENTIST

PLUMBER

SECRETARY

ASTRONAUT

CARTOON LETTERING FOR QUICK SKETCHES

Here is a good all-around cartoon lettering alphabet for quick sketch cartoons.

By the way, if you're working with a marker which can't be erased, be sure to check the correct spelling!

A SPECIAL THANKS TO ALL THE PEOPLE WHO GRACIOUSLY AGREED TO BE SUBJECTS IN THIS CHAPTER (IN ORDER OF APPEARANCE):

Peter Frattali
Marcia Wynn
Christine Duffy
Jason Campbell
Marisa Girgenti
Garvin Antoine
Theresa Conner
Anna Drakopoulos
Trudy Nash
David Maguire
Marg Newton
Jim Drakopoulos

Robert Fortunato
Robert Becker
Sal Italiano
Terrence Hussein
Alanna Blitz
Darrell Wong
Elliott Alexander
Eric Blitz
Mark Bell
Frances Blitz
Ryan Mennen

MY GOOD FRIEND CORY CRIVARI AND I TOOK ALL BUT ONE OF THE PHOTOS IN THIS CHAPTER.

CHALK TALK

Chalk Talk is a form of entertainment that goes back to the days of live stage shows, long before the days of movies, television, and even radio (although it would be pretty hard to draw cartoons over the radio). A chalk talk artist would recite a poem, story, or even sing a song while he drew quick cartoons in front of a live audience. These cartoons cleverly fit into the story and always had a trick or surprise ending. Chalk Talk is great fun for the artist to do, and fascinating for the audience to watch.

WHERE TO PERFORM CHALK TALK

Chalk Talk works great at schools, churches, parties, or even business meetings. It's a terrific way to get your message across in a fun and entertaining way.

WHAT YOU'LL NEED

1. AN EASEL—One that is tall—so that you can stand next to it—and sturdy enough to hold a large pad of paper.

2. PAD OF PAPER—When working in front of a large crowd, I use a pad of newsprint or drawing paper measuring at least 18" x 24". I have even used a pad as large as 24" x 36".

3. MARKERS, CHALK, AND CRAYON—The marker that you use must have a wide nib, so that the line is broad enough to be seen by everyone. Black shows up the best. Chalk or crayon is used for shading by laying it on its side to cover a large area at once; or it can be used for the actual outline of the sketch, instead of a marker.

In this chapter, I'll show you some of my favorite chalk talk stunts and doodle tricks so that you can get started giving your own chalk talk presentations.

HOW TO PERFORM A CHALK TALK PRESENTATION . . . AND HOW NOT TO

RIGHT

WRONG

TIPS:

1. Make bold, definite lines; not light, sketchy ones. Use broad, sweeping strokes.

2. Don't go too fast, thinking that you have to show them a zillion tricks. It's better to perform less doodle tricks . . . and do them well.

3. Speak up. Have a few cheerful greetings ready to loosen up the crowd, and as many jokes as you can come up with to liven up your presentation. After doing a few demonstrations, you'll know which ones work and which ones don't.

4. Have someone from the audience come up on stage to write a letter, word, or number for you to finish into a cartoon. This interaction works extremely well. They love to be involved!

5. Know the audience you are going to be drawing for, and tailor your material to fit the group.

6. For a great ending, draw a caricature (cartoon portrait) of someone in the audience, such as the teacher, principal, event organizer, or maybe even the person who was laughing the loudest. The rest of the audience loves to see someone they know get drawn.

Here is a drawing
shown actual size.

Use this to study
the boldness
of the marker
and the
sweeping
strokes
of the chalk.

ALPHABET LETTERTOONS

Turning letters into finished cartoons always amazes people.
This trick is a real crowd-pleaser!

A GOOD EXERCISE IS
TO GO THROUGH THE ALPHABET
AND CREATE A FEW DOODLES FOR
EACH LETTER. HEY, AT LEAST YOU'LL
LEARN YOUR A-B-C'S!

NUMBER TRICKS

3 DIGITS

KID DOING A HANDSTAND

SHEIK

MOTIVATIONAL TIP
Practice daily! Seven days without cartooning makes one WEAK.

SOME QUICKIES!

If you can spell the word DUCK, you can draw one.

DUCK

DUCK — I'M NOT A QUICKIE... ...I'M A QUACKIE!

JOY

JOY

From the word JOY . . .

To someone who gives you joy!

MOTIVATIONAL TIP
A little talent and hard work is worth more than a lot of talent and little effort.

UPSIDE-DOWN GAGS

To get the maximum effect out of these terrific surprise ending gags, it's best not to do them one right after the other. For the purpose of this book I've put them next to each other, but it is a good idea to slip a couple of number, letter, or word-doodle tricks in between these upside-down gags. The reason for this is because the audience begins to anticipate the ending by tilting their heads halfway through your presentation, and it ruins the surprise.

THE BAD BABY

With a little imagination, you could build this into a neat little story.

1. Start with a vegetable shape . . .
   a lima bean.

2. Add some detail to draw a baby.

3. Add more detail like
   hair, ears, and a bib.

4. Ask: "What happens
   to bad babies who don't
   eat their vegetables?"

5. Turn upside-down for the answer.

6. "They grow up to be mean men."

292

1. Once there was a man who was shipwrecked at sea. We'll draw his nose, his chin, and one of his eyes, which looks pretty sad.

2. We'll draw his mouth. Because it was a hot, desert island, he had to weave a hat of straw from the trees.

3. It's a good thing he did weave that hat, because as you can see from his long, white beard, he was there for a very long time.

4. But he never gave up hope that one day he would be rescued. He was rewarded for his great faith because one day a ship did come to rescue him.

5. Turn this drawing upside-down.

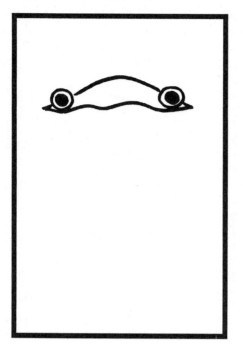

1. Draw two eyes and the top of a frog head. Add a mouth. Ask the crowd to call out what it is you are drawing once they recognize it.

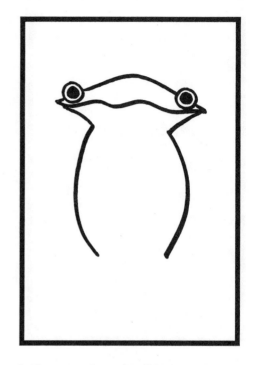

2. By now, they should recognize that it is a frog. You continue to draw the body.

3. We'll add the back legs and his feet.

4. Now we'll add some markings on his stomach. Ask the audience what always happens to the frog in every story. They will all say, "He turns into a prince!" Which, of course, is what happens when you turn this drawing upside-down.

1. Let's draw her eyes, eyelashes, and a small nose.

2. We'll add some lips. (Try not to close up the lines too much on her lips.) Add a facial outline.

3. Add a big head of curly hair.

4. Add a curl in her forehead, a comb in her hair, and a fancy collar.

5. Turn this drawing over to reveal a kindly old king.

MISCELLANEOUS DOODLE TRICKS

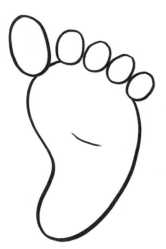

Taking care of five crying babies is a real FEET . . . er . . . FEAT!

Look what happens when a bee lands on a guy's face . . .

MOTIVATIONAL TIP
There are no shortcuts to any place worth going.

VISUAL GAGS

STEAMED CLAMS

HOW TO DO THEM

Visual gags can be very punny . . . er . . . I mean funny.

Puns are a natural for cartooning. Think of a well-known saying, expression, or word, and illustrate it to convey a different meaning.

ROLL MODEL

HARD TO PART WITH

CARTOONING PROJECTS

Here are some neat things to do with your cartoons.

MAKE GRANDPA SMILE . . . AND FROWN!

1. Draw a picture of Grandpa, as shown here, making sure that the eyebrows, mouth, and lower lip are straight across horizontally, showing no definite expression.

2. Fold down each side of the paper at the corners of Grandpa's mouth, as shown here.

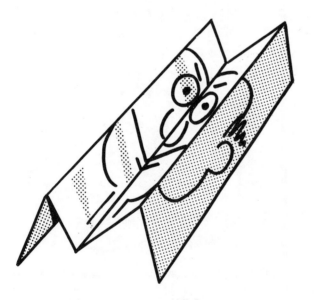

3. Make another fold down the center of your paper, so that from the side it creates the letter "M."

4. By looking directly into Grandpa's eyes and tilting the paper back and forth, he appears to smile and frown. The audience, too, always smiles at this one (but doesn't frown!).

THE SPAGHETTI EATER

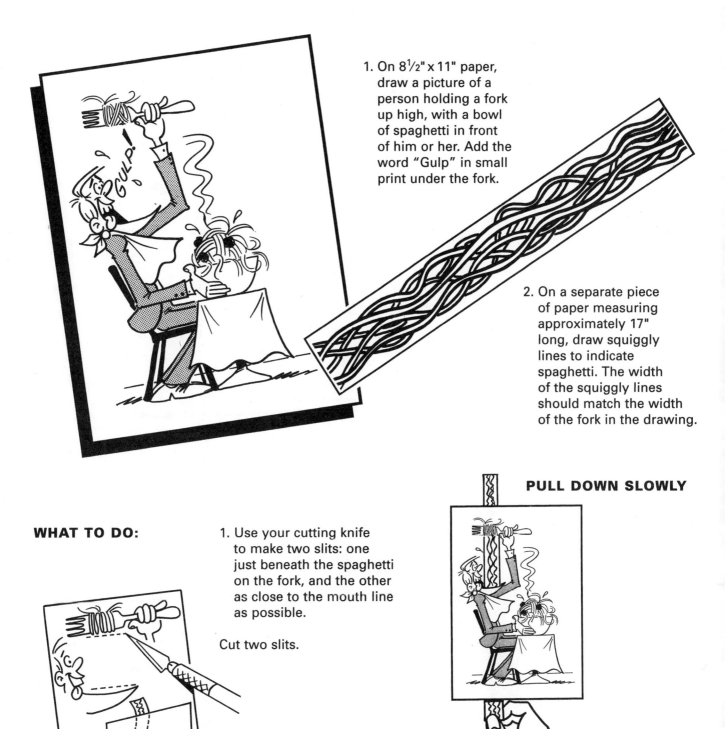

1. On 8½" x 11" paper, draw a picture of a person holding a fork up high, with a bowl of spaghetti in front of him or her. Add the word "Gulp" in small print under the fork.

2. On a separate piece of paper measuring approximately 17" long, draw squiggly lines to indicate spaghetti. The width of the squiggly lines should match the width of the fork in the drawing.

PULL DOWN SLOWLY

WHAT TO DO:

1. Use your cutting knife to make two slits: one just beneath the spaghetti on the fork, and the other as close to the mouth line as possible.

   Cut two slits.

2. Insert the spaghetti strip from the back through the top slit, down and in the bottom slit as shown here.

FRONT

THE EFFECT

Hold the bottom of the spaghetti strip and pull down slowly to make it look like he's eating a long, steady stream of spaghetti. When the strip is pulled out, it reveals the word "Gulp" for an added effect.

MAKE YOUR OWN GREETING CARDS

Here is a project that is fun to do with one of your animal sketches
(or any of your cartoons for that matter) . . . make your own greeting cards!

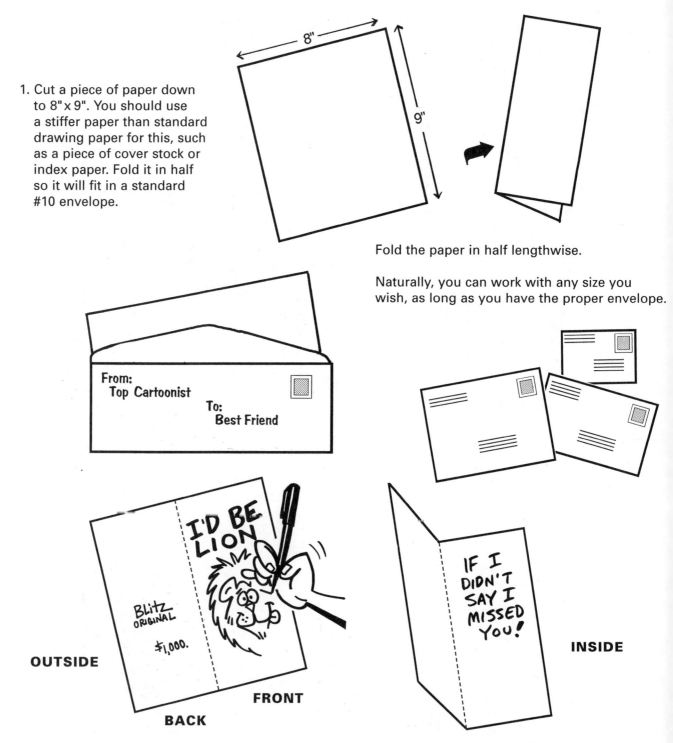

1. Cut a piece of paper down to 8" x 9". You should use a stiffer paper than standard drawing paper for this, such as a piece of cover stock or index paper. Fold it in half so it will fit in a standard #10 envelope.

Fold the paper in half lengthwise.

Naturally, you can work with any size you wish, as long as you have the proper envelope.

From:
Top Cartoonist
To:
Best Friend

I'D BE LION

BLitz ORIGINAL
$1,000.

OUTSIDE

FRONT

BACK

IF I DIDN'T SAY I MISSED YOU!

INSIDE

2. Draw your cartoon on the front, then write your name, the "price," or anything else you want on the back. This makes it more fun!

3. Write the punchline on the inside. Or, you may want to write the entire message on the front—it's up to you!

FLIP TIPS

I call this "flip tips" because we'll draw on the tips of a pad. Actually, on the lower corner. I think it is safe to assume that everyone has seen an animated cartoon at one time or another. As you may or may not know, it is done by drawing a series of drawings in a sequence to achieve the illusion of movement. For an eight-minute cartoon, it takes many thousands of drawings. For a feature-length movie, it's in the millions! But here, we'll use three drawings and we will still create movement in a "very short movie."

Title: "Pie in the Face"
Written, Directed &
Produced by: Bruce Blitz
(Music, too.)
Running time: 1 second

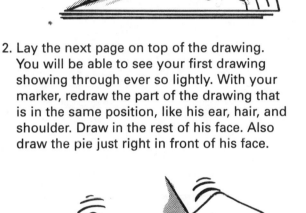

1. We will be working backwards. We'll start with the last drawing, so go 3 pages into your notepad and draw this fellow with a pie smashed in his face, complete with speed lines and sound effect. It's important to leave the pages connected to the pad, so don't tear them off. This way, the drawings will be "registered"—which means that they will always be in the same place.

2. Lay the next page on top of the drawing. You will be able to see your first drawing showing through ever so lightly. With your marker, redraw the part of the drawing that is in the same position, like his ear, hair, and shoulder. Draw in the rest of his face. Also draw the pie just right in front of his face.

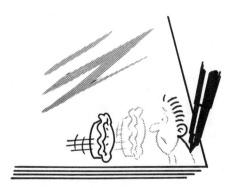

3. Flip the next page down on top of your second drawing. Redraw the whole face that you can see from the page below. Using the pie that you can faintly see as a guide, draw another pie further away from the man's face.

4. Take the top page in the left hand, the second page in your right hand, and view the three drawings in succession by using a rolling motion. If you want a bigger project, use the corners of an entire pad to create a longer sequence.

CARTOONING IS A FUNNY BUSINESS

If you are anything like me, you love drawing cartoons for the fun of it. But, imagine getting paid for your sketches! In many cases, a cartoonist can work anywhere—as long as he or she can mail or fax their drawings to prospective clients.

**CARTOONS
COMMAND
ATTENTION**

ATTENSHUN!

CARTOON

Cartooning can be a terrific source of fun and profit. I have found that good cartoonists are always in demand because cartoons are a great way to get a message across for advertising, greeting cards, newspaper editorials, book illustrations, animation, product design, and so on. Simply put, cartoons command attention!

There are tons of ways to earn money in cartooning, and in this chapter, I am going to show you a ton or two of them.

Computers

Sales • Service • Accessories

Here are examples of cartooning in business advertisements—these can be used as logos, storefront signs, newspaper ads, or business cards.

Animals are often linked with human emotions, traits, and clichés; and as such they can be very useful in advertising . . .

Happy as a **clam**

Gentle as a **lamb**

Strong as an **ox**

Silly as a **goose**

Slow as a **tortoise**

Elephants have great memories
The Lion is known as the King of the Jungle

MONARCH
Heating & Air
Conditioning

THE LIST GOES ON:

Sly as a **fox**
Wise as an **owl**
Quiet as a **mouse**
Eats like a **horse**
Bull in a china shop
Stubborn as a **mule**
Proud as a **peacock**
Peaceful as a **dove**
Playful as a **kitten**

Fierce as a **lion**
Graceful as a **swan**
Swift as a **deer**
Busy as a **bee**
Blind as a **bat**
Dog tired
Slippery as a **snake**
Monkey see, **monkey** do

TRY TO DRAW THESE YOURSELF!

307

HERE ARE THREE MORE "OPPORTOONITIES" . . .
HOW MANY MORE CAN YOU THINK OF?

PRODUCT GRAPHICS

T-SHIRTS ARE A POPULAR FORM OF ADVERTISING

GREETING CARD DESIGN

PRACTICE TIP #13

Look in the phone book
and make up sketches
to go with the listings.

EARN MONEY IN THE CARICATURE BIZ

There are numerous opportunities for earning money as a quick-sketch caricature artist.
Here are just some of the possibilities:

- Parties
- Conventions
- Trade Shows
- Vacation Resorts
- Amusement Parks
- Custom Gifts

A good caricature artist can keep a crowd fascinated for hours. Cartooning is a great source of entertainment at a party, and the guests even get to take home their own cartoon portrait. People love to see a cartoon portrait develop right before their eyes, especially when it is of someone they know. You, as the artist/entertainer, can enhance the fun by making jokes and kidding around with the subject and the rest of the crowd. You can make people laugh just as a stand-up comic does when he or she faces an audience—only your back is to them, and you're probably sitting down!

PARTIES

When working at parties, vacation resorts, and similar locales, you must be able to work quickly and effectively. Profile views are commonly used because they make it easier to achieve a likeness, and you can get to more people at a party. You may want to charge by the hour with a two-hour minimum. Figure out how many quick sketch portraits you can do in an hour, so that when you speak to a potential customer, you can give him or her an idea of the number of guests that can be drawn in a certain amount of time.

A promotional flyer and business card can help to attract business. It's a good idea to place a few samples of your work on the flyer and a caricature of yourself on the card. Be sure to keep a supply of both with you, especially when you are working. You can drum up a lot of business while people watch you draw.

FAIRS, VACATION RESORTS, AND SHOPPING MALLS

People love to take home souvenirs from their vacations and other adventures, and caricatures are lifelong mementos. Unlike parties where you charge by the hour, in these cases you will have to charge by the drawing. The price you charge will depend on where you are working and the type of customer. A good idea is to offer a range of prices based on whether you use color or black-and-white, provide a mat or frame for the final, or draw a frontal or profile view.

A great attention-getting marketing tool is a display of ten or so sample caricatures next to your easel. Make drawings of famous entertainers, politicians, sports figures, or anyone who is easily recognized. Be sure to keep your samples current. People just can't seem to pass by caricatures without attempting to name each one. Once there is a subject in your chair and you are drawing, you will soon be drawing a crowd of onlookers as well. As long as your work is good (and not offensive), you will surely have someone else sit down to be next. That's how it goes!

CONVENTIONS

Offering cartoon portraits at trade show booths, hospitality suites, and conventions is a great way for a company to give away a free gift to potential customers. The way it works is that you charge the company by the hour and you draw as many people as you can, taking ten minute breaks every hour. Sometimes, the company that hires you will request that you have their name or logo pre-printed on the paper so that the person will remember where they got it. Nothing draws a crowd of people to a trade show booth like a top-notch caricature artist! Contact various companies in your area to see if they attend trade shows, and send them your flyer or brochure.

MAIL ORDER

Caricatures by mail make terrific gifts, especially for the hard-to-buy-for person. Caricatures are personal, and they will be around for a long time. They are good for birthdays, anniversaries, retirements, graduations, and, of course, holidays.

As you can see from this sample flyer, the customer furnishes you with information such as eye color, hair color, subject's first name or nickname, and his or her sport, hobby, or business. It's also a good idea to specify on your printed material that the photo they submit must be clear and the subject's head be at least one inch tall. When you send the finished cartoon portrait to the customer, place it between two pieces of cardboard to protect it. You can charge a bit more for work of this kind because it usually will take more time than working from live subjects—and there is postage and handling involved.

CARICATURES MAKE GREAT SURPRISE GIFTS!

313

SELLING YOUR COMIC STRIP

SYNDICATES

To have your comic strip placed in the newspaper, you first have to send it to a syndicate and sell them on the idea of handling it. (Syndicates are the distributors who sell the feature to an editor who prints it in his or her newspaper.)

1. Send your comic strip to a syndicate.

2. If the syndicate decides to sell your strip, they will travel all over the country showing it to newspaper editors.

3. You can imagine how difficult this task would be for you to try on your own, with more than 1,500 newspapers in the United States alone . . .

. . . not to mention the trouble you would have simply getting an appointment to meet with one of these busy editors in the first place!

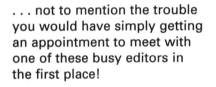

4. If the newspaper buys your comic strip, it then pays the syndicate, who in turn, splits that money with you—usually on a 50/50 basis. This can result in a great deal of money!

Persuading a syndicate to handle your strip is not an easy thing to do. And, like any other worthwhile venture, it requires persistence. Here are some guidelines to follow that will help you present yourself in a professional way:

Reduce 12 of your comic strips down to the size they would appear in the newspaper. Mount 3 or 4 of them on an 8½" x 11" sheet of paper. Be sure to put your name, address, and telephone number on each sheet.

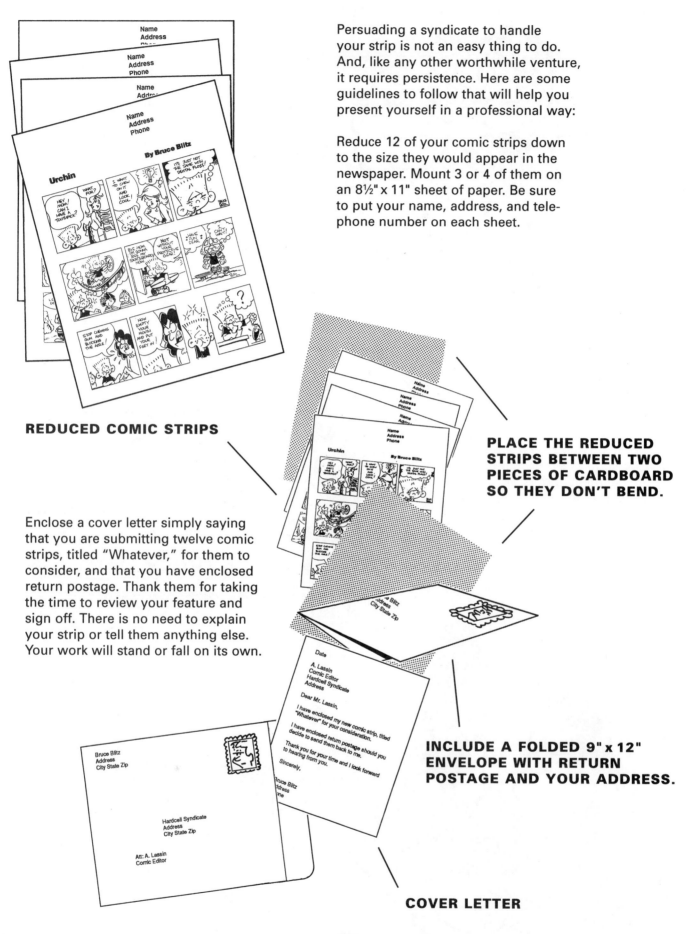

REDUCED COMIC STRIPS

Enclose a cover letter simply saying that you are submitting twelve comic strips, titled "Whatever," for them to consider, and that you have enclosed return postage. Thank them for taking the time to review your feature and sign off. There is no need to explain your strip or tell them anything else. Your work will stand or fall on its own.

PLACE THE REDUCED STRIPS BETWEEN TWO PIECES OF CARDBOARD SO THEY DON'T BEND.

INCLUDE A FOLDED 9" x 12" ENVELOPE WITH RETURN POSTAGE AND YOUR ADDRESS.

COVER LETTER

To obtain a list of the names and addresses of the syndicates, write to the following organization for a copy of their annual **Syndicate Directory**, which is available for a nominal fee:

Editor & Publisher
11 West 19th Street
New York, NY 10011-4234
Attention: Circulation Department
(212) 675-4380

If your strip is returned to you, simply send it right out to another syndicate—there are many different syndicates. Above all, do not take rejection personally. The syndicates invest a lot of time and money in selling a new strip. This means that they have to feel that it has a fighting chance. More likely than not, it is not your ability as an artist or writer that is in question, but the fact that they felt the strip's subject matter wouldn't appeal to a large enough audience, or that the subject matter could run out of fresh ideas quickly. This is why you see so many family, animal, and children strips in papers. Remember, the trick is to conform to what is established while bringing something new to it!

The important thing is . . . don't give up! Many of the cartoonists whose strips now appear in the newspaper had been plugging away at it for a long time before they hit!

I think it is important to understand just how difficult it is to sell your cartoons to a syndicate. Syndicates receive thousands of submissions each year—and with newspapers having only a certain amount of space in the comic section, they have to be extremely selective. However, don't neglect the many other avenues there are for getting your work published.

LOCAL PUBLICATIONS

Contact editors of local newspapers and try to sell them on the idea of running a continuing feature of yours that could be written and drawn to suit the needs of their publication. For example, a comic strip with a main character that solves local problems with which their readers can all identify. Or maybe a gag-a-day (-week or -month) panel that pokes fun at things in the community.

Don't be concerned with getting paid for this at first. It will be well worth it for the exposure, experience, and fun. The goal is to have your work in print! Later on, you may be able to use this published work to get cartooning jobs that pay!